Hobbyist Guide
—— To ——
Successful Koi Keeping

AQUARIUM DIGEST INTERNATIONAL
——— COLLECTOR'S EDITION ———

Hobbyist Guide
——— To ———
Successful Koi Keeping

Dr. David Pool

ACKNOWLEDGEMENTS

I would like to thank Mr Kenji Sakamoto of Tetra
Japan and Mr Nigel Caddock of Nishikigoi
International for their assistance in obtaining
photographic material for this book.

© 1991
Tetra-Press
TetraWerke Dr. rer nat. Ulrich Baensch GmbH
P.O.Box 1580. D-4520 Melle, Germany
All rights reserved, incl. film, broadcasting,
television as well as the reprinting
1st edition 1-10.000, 1991
Printed in Spain by Egedsa
DLB-30.313-91
Distributed in U.S.A. by
Tetra Sales (Division of Warner-Lambert)
Morris Plains, N.J. 07950
Distributed in UK by Tetra Sales, Lambert Court,
Chestnut Avenue, Bastleigh Hampshire S05 3ZQ
WL-Code: 16583

ISBN 3-89356-134-X

CONTENTS

Koi of the Ai-goromo variety

Dr. David Pool

INTRODUCTION

The keeping of Nishikigoi, or koi, first began in the early 19th Century with the advent of coloured mutations of the common carp, Cyprinus carpio. These first koi, kept by Japanese farmers in the Niigata region of Japan, were probably produced largely by accident, but since that time selective breeding has resulted in the bright colouration and numerous varieties that are available today.

Koi keeping is becoming increasingly popular throughout the world, with many people every year starting in this fascinating pastime and enjoying the grace and beauty of these fish. The depth to which koi keepers become involved in their hobby varies greatly. For some people koi keeping involves the addition of one or two koi into a garden pond. For others it involves the construction of a purpose built koi pond and exhibiting their prize individuals at the large shows which are held every year.

This handbook has been produced for koi keepers at all levels. It's aim is to provide guidelines for maintaining koi in order that they can be kept in the best possible conditions and develop to their full potential.

David Pool

Good water quality is essential if a koi is to be at its best. This high quality Taisho Sanke would not look as impressive if kept in poor water quality conditions.

THE IMPORTANCE OF WATER QUALITY

The importance of good water quality when keeping koi cannot be overestimated and the saying amongst koi keepers that "if you look after the water, the koi will look after themselves" is undoubtedly true. In fact over 80% of the problems encountered by koi keepers can be traced directly or indirectly to poor water quality. These problems range from poor colouration, lethargy and increased disease susceptibility to direct toxicity. Fortunately most water quality troubles can be easily corrected or better still prevented, particularly if you have a basic understanding of what is happening in the pond. The following aspects of water quality are those most likely to cause problems in a pond:

Temperature
pH and hardness
Ammonia, nitrite and nitrate
Chlorine and chloramine

Temperature

Koi are cold-blooded, which means that their body temperature is very close to the temperature of the water that they live in. Consequently all of their behaviours are affected by the temperature of the pond. All koi keepers will have seen the effects of temperature on the feeding of their koi, but all of the other bodily functions are also affected. Koi can survive at temperatures ranging from 0-35°C, however at either extreme the koi will be very lethargic, stop feeding, be susceptible to disease etc. Even at more favourable temperatures the koi are affected. For example at temperatures below 12°C their immune system is very inactive, and below 6°C the koi will rarely feed. The "ideal" temperature range for koi is from 15-25°C when their bodily functions will be at their most effective, although their colouration is improved as the temperature drops.

To avoid temperature related problems in the pond, extreme values should be avoided. The upper temperature limits (ie above 30°C) are unlikely to occur in most koi ponds, but if they do, shading the pond using garden netting, a pergola or other cover, will help.

At high temperatures, low oxygen levels may occur in the water, therefore good aeration using airstones, a venturi, fountain, etc, is important. Low temperatures are more of a problem to the koi and koi keeper. The low temperatures (below 4°C) can be avoided by ensuring that the pond is at least 120cm

p.10/11: Many koi don't conform to any particular vainety, but are still attractive.

Building a koi pond within a conservatory ensures that the water temperature does not fall too low in the winter and keeps the koi active throughout the year.

deep and avoiding excess water circulation. This will allow a warm layer of water to settle on the pond bottom where the koi will congregate.

To avoid disturbing this layer, water pumps should be turned down and positioned so that they take water from the surface and create little turbulence. If this is not possible the pump should be switched off - more problems will be caused by circulating the water and allowing it all to drop to levels approaching 0°C, than would be caused by the minute amounts of pollutants produced by the dormant fish which will, in any event, be decomposed by bacteria within the pond. A more costly alternative that will allow you to maintain the temperature at favour-

able levels, is to install a large pool heater (eg a swimming pool heater) or position the pond in a summer house or conservatory. Although expensive, these latter measures keep your koi active throughout the year.

Perhaps as important as preventing extreme values is the necessity to avoid sudden changes in temperature, which will stress the fish making them susceptible to disease. Early spring and late autumn are times when sudden changes may occur, due to the hot days and very cold nights. Such problems are mainly a problem in shallow ponds which are most affected by air temperature. Equally, care should be taken when undertaking larger partial water changes.

pH and Hardness

The pH of the water is a measure of its acidity or alkalinity and the values range from pH 1 (acidic) through pH 7 (neutral) to pH 14 (alkaline). Hardness is a measure of the dissolved metal salts in the water and is measured in degrees of German Hardness (°dH).

The more salts there are the harder the water. Hardness is often divided into general hardness, which measures the amount of calcium and magnesium salts, and carbonate hardness which measures the amount of carbonate and bicarbonate salts. Carbonate hardness buffers the water against sudden changes in pH.

Within sensible limits the pH and hardness of the water are not critical for koi and they will happily survive in pH values ranging from 6.5 - 8.5 and hardness values from 2 - 20°dH. In fact in a pond containing dense algal or plant growth the pH will change considerably in a diurnal pattern. The plants and algae use up the bicarbonates which buffer the pH and during the night they respire, producing carbon dioxide which causes the pH to drop. During the day they photosynthesise (use carbon dioxide and water to produce carbohydrates and oxygen) using up any carbon dioxide and allowing the water to return to its natural pH. Therefore the pH at dawn is likely to be considerably lower than at dusk. However, because the change occurs slowly, it does not harm the fish.

If the pH or hardness of the pond

High pH values in the pond are usually due to the water being in contact with unsealed cement or lime rich stones.

In the fall, leaves will accumulate in the pond and can lead to pollution.

water are outside the limits described above it may be necessary to alter the water quality. Wherever possible you should locate the cause of the change and remove it rather than trying to alter the quality of the water itself. A sudden rise or a high pH often results from the water coming into contact with untreated cement or limestone. This may be present in the pond or in the surrounds. Use of a commercially available sealant on cement in the pond and ensuring water drains away from the pond will overcome the problem. A drop in pH may be caused by a build up of organic debris, garden run off, heavy rainfall or perhaps a malfunctioning filter.

Regularly monitoring the water using Tetra pH and Hardness Test Kits will enable unsuitable or changing pH values to be detected quickly and easily. In ponds containing excess algae or plants pH tests should be conducted at the same time of day on each occasion in order to prevent any variation due to the diurnal pattern. Immediately after building and following any alterations to the pond or surroundings, the water should be tested at 2 or 3 day internals.

In an established pond, weekly testing is sufficient. It is also advisable to test the tap water before a large partial water change is conducted to ensure that it is similar to that in the pond. As with temperature a sudden change in pH is more dangerous than a slightly unsuitable but constant value.

The following table gives some indication of how to adjust the pH and hardness in the pond should this be necessary. Always conduct such changes slowly over a period of days to avoid stressing the fish unnecessarily.

Problem	Cause	Correction
pH and hardness too high (pH > 8.5 hardness > 20°dH)	Limestone rocks in pond Unsealed cement Run off from surrounds Hard alkaline tapwater	Remove rocks Treat all cement Divert away from pond Dilute tapwater with soft, acidic rainwater or use commercial pH adjusters.
pH and hardness too low (pH <6.5 hardness <2°dH)	Excess organic debris Filter malfunction Excess rainwater Soft acidic tapwater	Remove regularly Check filter Divert away from pond Add a small amount of limestone to pond or filter or use commercial pH adjusters.

The Nitrogen Cycle

Within the pond or aquarium, fish waste together with any uneaten food, dead plants or algae is decomposed in a process known as the nitrogen cycle.

This involves the breakdown of the fish waste into ammonia or ammonium, nitrite and finally nitrate. Each of these stages is accomplished by bacteria in the presence of oxygen.

The first stage in the nitrogen cycle is the formation of ammonia (toxic) or ammonium (non toxic). Ammonia and ammonium are easily converted into the other, with the rela-

tive amounts of each being largely dependent upon pH. At high pH values (greater than 8.5) the water contains large amounts of ammonia, whereas at lower pH values it contains mainly ammonium.

An ammonia concentration of only 0.01 to 0.02mg per litre of water can cause problems to the koi. Fortunately this level of ammonia is unlikely to be reached in most koi ponds due to their pH being less than 8.0.

Ammonia is converted into nitrite by Nitrosomonas bacteria. Nitrites are less toxic than ammonia, but wherever possible the concentration

15

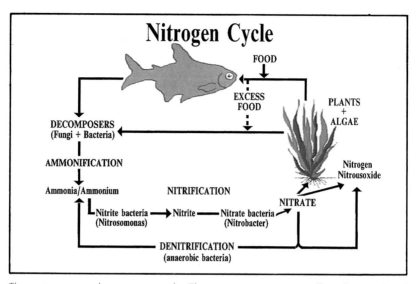

The main steps in the nitrogen cycle. This process occurs naturally in the pond and filter resulting in the decomposition of organic matter.

in the pond or aquarium water should be kept below 0.2mg nitrite per litre of water. Raised levels indicate a breakdown in the biological filtration system, excess debris, overfeeding or overcrowding.

Nitrite is finally converted into nitrate by Nitrobacter bacteria. Nitrates are much less toxic and are used by algae and plants as a source of nutrition. The nitrate levels in a koi pond will gradually increase due to it being constantly produced by the biological filter. At raised levels it will encourage rapid growth of algae and at levels of 50mg nitrate per litre of water will start to adversely affect the koi.

High concentrations of ammonia, nitrite and nitrate may affect the delicate skin and gill membranes of the fish causing irritation, excess production of mucus and in some cases damage. In addition nitrites can bind with the haemoglobin in the fish's blood reducing its ability to carry oxygen.

The effects of raised levels of these pollutants are that the fish rub against underwater objects, have a slimy appearance to the skin and show signs of oxygen shortage, eg gasping at the surface, rapid gill movements and accumulating around the filter outflow. At high concentrations, the kidney may be damaged affecting the water balance of the fish and resulting in extreme cases in dropsy and pop-eye. Other signs include reduced growth rates, listless behaviour and greatly increased susceptibility to disease.

The sumi (black colouration) of this Shiro Bekko is affected by the pH of the water, being more intense in slightly alkaline water.

A venturi draws air into the water returning to the pond from the filter.

Regularly monitoring the ammonia, nitrite and nitrate levels in the pond using the relevant Tetra test kits will enable you to detect raised levels before they adversely affect the fish. In a well established pond, where the bacteria in the filter receive an adequate supply of oxygen rich water, they should never reach toxic levels, although weekly water testing is advisable.

This is not the case if the pond or filter have recently been installed or cleaned. Here there are too few bacteria present to complete each stage or the nitrogen cycle and toxic levels of ammonia or nitrite may occur.

Similarly, if the fish are overfed, large numbers of new fish are added or debris falls into the pond, there will be a period when there are insufficient bacteria to decompose the increased amount of organic mate-

rial and raised levels of ammonia and nitrite will occur. When high levels are recorded a partial water change should immediately be undertaken and any excess debris removed. This will reduce the pollutant concentration providing a temporary respite while the cause of the problem is located.

To prevent a recurrence of the problem the feeding rates and stocking level should be checked and reduced if too high, the filter should be checked and cleaned if necessary and the overall pond hygiene improved. The nitrate level may be reduced by undertaking regular partial water changes, although the level in the tap-water should be checked beforehand. Alternatively a vegetable filter may be installed. Active filter media such as zeolite are also ideal for quickly removing ammonia from the water.

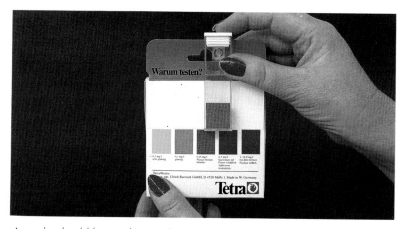

A test kit should be used routinely to monitor the water quality within your koi pond.

It is important to note that in the absence of oxygen, nitrates are converted into toxic nitrites and ammonia. Therefore it is important that the biological filtration does not become blocked with debris or accidentally switched off for any length of time (except possibly in winter at temperatures below 6°C).

Chlorine and Chloramine

Most koi keepers use tap-water to fill their ponds and aquaria. It is important to remember that tap-water is produced for human consumption and as such contains disinfectants such as chlorine and chloramine to remove any harmful bacteria which may be present. Unfortunately the chlorine and chloramine can also harm the fish and in particular, kill the helpful filter bacteria. Therefore whenever conducting a water change of more than 10% of the pond volume, a good quality water conditioner such as TetraPond AquaFin should be used. For smaller water changes, the tap water should be sprayed onto the pond, as much of the chlorine will readily dissipate in the process. What chlorine remains will be greatly diluted in the pond. Never place the tap-water directly into the filter as even the low chlorine levels remaining may harm the filter bacteria. If chloramine is present in the tapwater, spraying will not reduce its concentration and a water conditioner should always be used.

Oxygen

Oxygen in the pond is vital for the survival of both fish and filter bacteria. The oxygen is absorbed into the water at the surface and this can be greatly improved by ensuring good circulation and turbulence.

This may be achieved using a venturi attached to the filter outflow, airstones or some form of waterfall. These methods of water circulation are particularly important on hot, still nights when oxygen levels in the pond may drop. Oxygen levels in the filter should be maximised by the use of spray bars, airstones, or similar equipment to ensure that the bacteria work at their optimum levels.

Pollutants

There are numerous pollutants which may accidentally contaminate the pond and adversely affect the fish. Pesticides used in the garden are one obvious source. They should always be kept away from the pond and not used when the wind may blow them onto the water. Also ensure that water running off the surrounding ground does not enter the pond. Certain trees and shrubs have leaves which are toxic to the fish. Laburnum is one notable example and should always be kept away from the pond. Finally, there are pollutants which may enter the pond on your hands. Suntan oils, perfumes and other chemicals can be accidentally introduced into the pond in this way and may harm the fish.

The importance of maintaining good water quality has been stressed in the preceding paragraphs. Ensuring good conditions is relatively easy, involving regular water testing, partial water changes, together with sensible filter and pond maintenance.

Such tasks only take a few minutes each week, but are well worth the effort involved with the rewards being in the form of trouble free fishkeeping and healthy koi.

page 20/21: Crystal clear water will allow your fish to be seen at their best. (Photograph Kahl).

POND FILTRATION

The importance of maintaining good water quality, with a low level of pollutants was stressed in the previous chapter.

In a pond containing few fish and many plants or algae this is achieved naturally. However, for most koi keepers, where the pond is more heavily stocked and there are few plants, it is necessary to artificially maintain good conditions by undertaking regular, large partial water changes or, more usually, by installing a filter.

Before examining the types of filters suitable for use in a koi pond it is useful to understand the principles which they utilise.

Principles of Filtration

The basic principles of filtration are the same whether the filter is being used in a pond or aquarium. There are four main forms of filtration.

Healthy koi and crystal clear water, the result of effective filtration.

Mechanical Filtration

In mechanical filtration any particles in the water are removed. This may be achieved by using a filter medium which acts like a sieve and strains out particulate matter, or by allowing the particles to settle to the bottom of a container from where they can be removed.

For relatively small ponds, foam or filter brushes are often used to mechanically strain the water. In this situation the finer the filter medium, the more effective it will be at removing debris' but unfortunately it will also easily become blocked and require regular cleaning if it is to remain efficient.

Settlement chambers are usually incorporated into larger filters. These chambers greatly slow down the water flow allowing particulate matter to sink. Their efficiency is improved by adding filter brushes or baffles which will further reduce water turbulence. The surface (= clearest) water from the settlement chamber should be directed into the next part of the filter.

The settlement principle has been taken one stop further in the "Vortex" chambers used in larger koi ponds. Water from the pond is directed into the cylindrical/cone shaped unit to create a whirlpool. In this situation debris accumulates in the centre of the whirlpool and slowly sinks to the bottom from where it can be removed. The clear water from the centre of the whirlpool at the top is passed into the next

stage of the filter. Mechanical filtration relies on large particles of debris being strained out of or settling from the water. The pump which powers the filter should ideally not be positioned in front of the mechanical filter, since it will break up any debris making it more difficult to remove mechanically.

A vortex unit (in the foreground) allows sediment to settle out of the water before it enters the biological filter. (Photograph courtesy of Nishikigoi International).

Sand pressure filters are a specialised form of mechanical filter in which fine sand is used to remove any particulate matter present in the water. To reduce the incidence of blockage and to allow larger volumes of water to be filtered, these filters use water which is pumped through at a high pressure (generated using a suitable external pump). Regular backwashing, ie reversing

Sand pressure filters enable fine particulate matter to be removed from the water. (Photograph courtesy of Nishikigoi International).

the flow of water through the sand and discarding the dirty water, ensures that the sand does not become blocked. Sand pressure filters are always positioned after the main pond filter so that they do not receive coarse suspended debris. If used they will remove fine particles and result in the water appearing very clear. Sand pressure filters also act as a biological filter, although this is not their main function.

Biological Filtration

A biological filter is the site where the bacteria which consumes organic waste are encouraged to grow. The biological filter does not just contain bacteria, there are also numerous fungi, worms, snails,

25

crustacea and algae, all of which help in decomposing fish waste and other organic debris. However, it is the Nitrosomonas and Nitrobacter bacteria which complete the major steps in the decomposition of organic material as described in the previous chapter.

In order to encourage a good growth of bacteria it is important to provide a large surface area for them to grow on and an abundant oxygen supply. The oxygen is provided by having a good flow of water through the filter medium. To ensure that the water is saturated with oxygen it may, for example, be directed onto the filter media through a spray bar, or airstones may be positioned in the water before the biological filter.

A multichamber filter with hair rollers, foam and gravel as a filter medium. (Photograph courtesy of John Cuvelier)

The choice of filter medium has to provide the large surface area required by the bacteria to grow on, but also reduce the possibility of blockage or preventing a good flow of oxygen rich water. Fine gravel or sand, for example, would provide a very large surface area but because they become blocked easily and would restrict the flow of water, oxygen would only reach the surface layers with the rest of the media being ineffective.

A wide range of materials are used for biological filtration including foam, hair rollers, plastic tubing, gravel and fibrous matting. Whichever media is chosen it is pointless having a great depth in the filter. This is because bacteria close to the water inflow will use up oxygen resulting in there being less available deeper in the media. Therefore the bacteria deeper in the media will be less efficient and this part of the filter will, in effect, be wasted. The amount of media to use depends on the material in question, the water flow through it and the oxygen content of the water. As an example, if gravel is chosen as a filter medium, a maximum depth of 15-20cm should be used.

Biological filtration in a pond is greatly affected by water temperature. In general, as the water temperature increases the bacteria become more active and so more effective at decomposing any organic waste products. In the winter, the bacteria sill function, but at a much

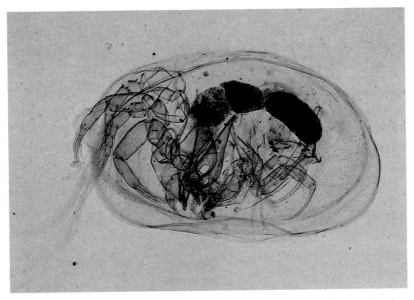

The biological filter contains many life forms other than bacteria. Ostracods (above left) and Nematodes (above right) consume bacteria and other organic material, helping to prevent the filter clogging. (Photograph courtesy of J Chubb)

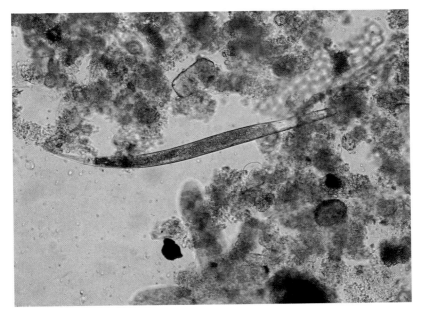

slower rate. Fortunately at these low temperatures there is little fish waste produced therefore the filter bacteria can still maintain good water quality. Below 6°C the bacteria and fish are very inactive and many koi keepers switch off the filter without any adverse effects on the water quality. When the filter is switched on again raised levels of ammonia and nitrite may occur, therefore these values should be monitored using a test kit. Removing excess debris from the filter when it is switched off will help to minimise such problems.

Chemical Filtration

Chemical media such as zeolite can be used in the filter to actively remove certain harmful compounds. If used they should be placed after the biological filter, where they will remove some of the ammonia not consumed by the bacteria. If placed in front of the biological filter, the zeolite will remove the food source of the bacteria.

The larger the surface area of the zeolite in contact with the water, the more effective it will be at removing pollutants. In practise the ideal particle size is 5-10cm diameter as this prevents excessive compacting which would prevent the water flowing over the media.

In a well managed established pond, chemical filtration should not be required as the biological filter should be able to maintain very low pollutant levels. However if the pond is overstocked, overfed, new fish are added, or the bacteria are not functioning effectively (eg if the filter is blocked or recently set up), the chemical media will help to prevent a potentially lethal build up of toxic pollutants.

Chemical media work by actively absorbing certain chemicals from the water. There are a limited number of sites where this absorbtion can occur and so eventually the chemical media will become exhausted. This may take from a few days to several months depending on the quantities of pollutants in the water. Chemical media in a polluted or recently set up pond will rapidly become exhausted, whereas in a well maintained, established pond with a good biological filter they will last much longer.

Zeolite also removes remedies from the water and should therefore be removed before water of disease treatments are added. Once exhausted the chemical filter will simply act as a surface for bacteria to grow on. Regular monitoring of the ammonia and nitrite levels using a Tetra Test Kit may show a slight rise in concentration when the media becomes exhausted and need reactivating.

Zeolite can be reactivated by placing it in a concentrated salt solution (6g of cooking salt per litre of water) for 24 to 48 hours and then carefully rinsing in freshwater before replacing in the filter.

Vegetable Filtration

A biological filter will decompose organic material and produce nitrates. In a natural pond with large quantities of healthy plants, these nitrates will be used as a food source and removed from the water. However, in a koi pond, where there are few if any plants, the nitrates may be used as a food source by algae which will multiply rapidly resulting in "green water" or dense growths of blanketweed. Alternatively, if the algae are being controlled in some way, the nitrate concentration in the pond may increase rapidly and adversely affect the fish.

Adding fast growing pond plants (eg Elodea) will reduce the nitrate level. However, this is not feasible if large koi are kept in the pond as they will uproot and consume the plants. In this situation a vegetable filter is ideal. This involves adding fast growing plants (eg watercress) to the last chamber of the filter or to a causeway carrying water from the filter back to the pond. The watercress will grow very rapidly using up large quantities of nitrates (and other nutrients required by the algae to grow) and maintain clear water of good quality. The watercress will require regular pruning to remove any esccess growth.

Ultraviolet Light Units

Ultraviolet (UV) light was first used by pondkeepers as a means of controlling parasites. For this purpose it is of limited use in a single koi pool, since some parasites will always find a new host before they pass through the UV unit. However, UV light also kills suspended algae and is now widely used as a means of maintaining clear water in the pond. Ideally the UV unit should be situated after the filter so that it is not affected by water borne debris. The nitrate concentration in the pond should be monitored using a Tetra Nitrate Test Kit as it may rise rapidly when there are no algae present to utilise it. The use of a vegetable filter is the ideal solution to such potential problems. If a vegetable filter is not used blanketweed will often grow to take advantage of the of the rich supply of nutrients. UV units are available in a range of sizes for use in ponds of different volumes. Your local dealer will be able to provide advice on which UV unit will be most suitable for your particular pond.

Type of Pump

There is a bewildering choice of pumps which may be used in a koi pond to power the filter, venturi, waterfall, etc. the following section will provide some guidelines, but is also advisable to discuss your requirements with a reputable dealer. The initial choice is between a submersible and an external pump. As the name implies submersible pumps are placed in the water which prevent them overheating. For this reason they should never be operated out of the water as they will quickly overheat and become damaged. The choice is largely a personal one and will depend on the design of your pond. Submersible pumps for example are difficult to conceal if placed directly in the pond. In many cases they are positioned within a multi-chambered filter, although this is only possible if the filter is gravity fed (see section on filtration). External pumps should be positioned outside the pond in a well ventilated dry con-

External pumps should be placed in a waterproof container to protect them from water. (Photograph courtesy of John Cuvelier).

tainer. Although more difficult to install, they are ideal where continual operation over a long period of time is required.

The size of the pump is determined largely by the size of the pond in which it will be used, the height to which the water must be pumped and, to a lesser extent, the numbers and size of fish being kept. As a rough guide you should aim to pass the pond water through the filter once every 1 to 3 hours. If the filter is positioned well above the pond a more powerful pump will be required to provide the necessary water flow.

The details of pump outflow given by the manufacturers may be misleading. The flow rates given are usually those for a pump without any attached pipework. When the pipework necessary for the filter is added the outflow from the pump may be reduced by up to 20%. These losses can be minimised by installing pipework with a suitable diameter and avoiding unnecessary restrictions or bends.

The pump is the most important part of your koi pond system, providing a continual supply of water for the filter, aeration and water flow. It is therefore advisable to select a good quality pump which will perform these tasks reliably. It is also advisable to select a pump with an adjustable output. This will allow the water flow through the filter to be altered when required (seasonally, during maintenance, etc).

A vegetable filter containing watercress formed in a water course leading from the filter to the pond.

Whichever pump you select it is important to ensure that it is safe. Always follow the manufacturers instructions and use waterproof connections where required, together with an approved circuit breaker (which will automatically cut off the power should there be any damage to the pump or cable).

Types of Pond Filters

Having examined the principles of pond filtration we can now examine the different types of filter available and their suitability for different ponds.

Undergravel Filtration

An undergravel filter uses a bed of gravel within the pond as a filter medium. A series of perforated pipes are positioned under the gravel and water is drawn through them and the gravel by means of a pump (usually submersible). The gravel itself acts as both a mechanical and biological filter. For maximum efficiency you should aim to have a good network of perforated pipes and a gravel depth of 15-20cm. A greater depth of gravel does not improve the filter efficiency as there is insufficient oxygen in the lower layers for the bacteria to function. Regular cleaning (by stirring the gravel) is advisable to prevent it from becoming blocked and therefore less efficient. To further reduce blockage and to prevent excessive digging by the koi, 1cm diameter gravel should be used.

The size of the undergravel filter depends largely on the fish you intend to keep. In a planted pond only 20-25% of the bottom area may be used as a filter - do not plant in the gravel as it will block the filter making it less efficient. In a koi only pond the entire bottom may be used for the filter, although usually only 33-50% is utilised.

ADVANTAGES: Undergravel filters have a large amount of filter medium resulting in efficient filtration. They are also positioned in the pond and therefore do not take up space in the surrounding area.

DISADVANTAGES: Undergravel filters for ponds are rarely available commercially and so have to be constructed from PVC pipe. They also draw debris into the gravel, which may then be disturbed by the fish. Regular maintenance will prevent this, but is more difficult than for other filter types. Finally, other filter media (eg Zeolite) cannot easily be used in conjunction with an undergravel filter.

Reverse Flow Undergravel Filtration

Perhaps the major disadvantage of an undergravel filter is that debris is drawn into the gravel causing it to be become blocked and less efficient (within 4-6 weeks if not maintained correctly). This can be overcome by using reverse flow undergravel filtration.

In this method the pump passes the pond water through an external filter which mechanically removes any particulate matter and then into the perforated pipes and up through the gravel.

The external mechanical filter (eg a box filter filled with foam or a settlement chamber) requires regular maintenance, although this is a simple and quick process. The gravel acts as a very large biological filter and rarely becomes clogged and so only occasionally requires maintenance (= stirring and siphoning).

ADVANTAGES: Reverse flow undergravel filtration has all of the advantages of a standard undergravel filtration, but is also easier to maintain and does not accumulate the debris where it can be disturbed by the fish.

DISADVANTAGES: The major disadvantage is that such systems are rarely available commercially. Also debris may tend to accumulate on the gravel bed instead of settling in the deepest part of the pond, from where it can be easily removed or pumped into the filter.

The pumps in both types of undergravel filters must be kept running continually as, if switched off for any length of time, the bacteria in the gravel will die and pollute the water.

Internal Foam/Box Filters

Such filters generally use foam as a medium, either placed over the pump inflow or in a small canister. They are only suitable for small, lightly stocked ponds. In most cases they tend to be quite bulky and so look unsightly in a small pond or take up much water space.

Maintenance involves removing the foam filter, which acts mechanically and biologically and rinsing in old pond water. Do not use tapwater as the chlorine may kill the helpful bacteria.

ADVANTAGES: Internal filters are very easy to install in the pond and will run off a small pump, which is often incorporated in the filter making them suitable for the smaller ponds. They are inexpensive when compared to other filters.

DISADVANTAGES: These filters are often too small to be effective in medium sized or well stocked ponds. The foam tends to clog very quickly and although maintenance is easy, it involves reaching into the pond and disturbing plants, etc , when removing the filter. Such filters are not suitable for permanent koi ponds but are useful in a small quarantine or treatment ponds and containers.

External Filters

External filters are undoubtedly the most popular for all types of pond, ranging from a small pool to one in which large numbers of koi are kept. The external filters used by most koi keepers are comprised of a plastic box of a size suitable for the pond, which is filled with a series of foam sheets or similar filter medium. Water is pumped into the box by a

Filter brushes help to remove particulate matter during the mechanical section of the filtration. (Photograph courtesy of R Cleaver)

submerged or external pump. In the top of the filter it passes through a spray bar to oxygenate the water and then down through the filter medium before passing out of the filter and returning to the pond. The actual design of these box filters varies slightly depending on the manufacturer. In some the outflow from the filter is positioned so that the box is always full of water. In others where there is a large outflow pipe at the bottom of the box, the water flows back to the pond by gravity and the media are surrounded by air. Known as trickle filtration, this ensures the water is saturated with oxygen resulting in excellent bacterial growth. In a trickle filter more of the medium receives oxygenated water therefore a greater depth may

be used. As a result a well designed trickle filter can be deeper and considerable smaller than the equivalent standard box filter.

The basic external box filter may be greatly improved by a few additions. For example:

1. The water may first be passed through a settlement area (eg brushes) to remove any particulate matter before the biological filtration.

2. Zeolite may be placed after the biological media in order to remove any excess ammonia from the water.

3. An ultraviolet sterilising unit may be added to the pipework entering or leaving the filter in order to kill

any algae and keep the water clear. Maintenance of an external box filter is relatively easy, involving the removal of the upper foam sheets, which are then rinsed in old pond water. If other media are used they should be stirred and the dirty water drained to waste. Occasionally the pipework may also require cleaning using a pipe brush to ensure a good water flow. The water flow out of such a filter will give an indication of when cleaning is necessary. If the water flow decreases, the media is probably blocked and requires maintenance.

ADVANTAGES: An external box filter is very efficient if the size suitable for your pond is selected. They are also very flexible in that a range of different filter media may be used if required. Maintenance is straightforward. Finally they are available commercially.

DISADVANTAGES: The only minor dis-advantages with an external filter is that it can look unsightly positioned on the side of the pond. Some form of camouflage is therefore necessary.

Multichamber External Filters

The multichambered external filter is generally used for medium or larger koi ponds. In such a filter each chamber has a separate function. For example pond water may first pass into a settlement chamber with brushes, or into a vortex unit in order to remove any suspended particles. The clear water then passes into a biological filter chamber. Several chambers for biological filtration may be used in larger ponds. In each case the water passing from one chamber to the next is aerated to re-oxygenate it. To ensure that the maximum amount of filter medium is utilised in each chamber, water passes in at the top on one side and out at the bottom of the opposite side (or vice versa).

By using several relatively shallow chambers containing biological media rather than one deep one there will be fewer "dead" areas in the filter (ie where no aerobic bacteria exist due to the lack of oxygen), therefore the filter will be more efficient. The final chamber of the filter may contain zeolite and/or be used as a vegetable filter. A sand pressure filter may be added at the end of the filtration system in order to remove any small particles in the water and make it very clear.

Maintenance of multichamber filters is often simplified by the installation of drains in each chamber. In this way any debris which has accumulated may be washed away. Obviously where biological media are present it has to be retained by a plastic (or similar) mesh to prevent it being sucked into the drain.

Some koi keepers recommend that the water should always pass up through the biological media in chambers incorporating a drain at the bottom. In this situation debris would accumulate in the lower layers of the gravel and would be sucked out when the chamber is drained. Other koi keepers prefer water to flow onto the biological media at the top. In this case the media is stirred and the disturbed debris siphoned off.

In the preceding paragraphs the range of filters available for a pond and their relative advantages and disadvantages have been examined. The final choice is the pondkeepers and will depend on the pond size, space available, fish being kept and cost. Your local koi dealer or water garden centre should be able to demonstrate some of the filters described in this article and give you advice relating to your particular pond. Your dealer's advice will prove invaluable and will help to ensure that you select and install a suitable filter in the correct way.

A large Aka Matsuba koi such as this requires good pond conditions to remain at it's best.

KOI NUTRITION

The koi which you maintain in your aquarium or pond are reliant upon you to provide them with a suitable diet. It is important that this diet is nutritionally balanced in order to ensure that the koi remain healthy and grow. In this chapter the dietary requirements of koi will be examined and by understanding these some of the often quoted rules of when and what to feed the fish will be explained.

A Balanced Diet

Koi like most animals require a nutritionally balanced diet in order to grow and be in their best possible condition.

By this we mean that they require the correct amounts (and quality) of proteins, carbohydrates, fats, minerals and vitamins. The relative amounts of each of these nutrients required in the diet varies depending on water temperature, size of fish,

TABLE 1

NUTRIENTS REQUIRED IN A BALANCED DIET

Nutrient	Composition	Use in Body	Examples
Protein	Various combinations of 23 amino acids, 13 of which are essential for the Koi.	Form or repair body tissue and for inefficient energy production Cannot be stored	Meat and Fish
Carbo-hydrate	Generally formed by plants from carbon hydrogen and oxygen	Energy production. Excess stored in muscle and liver	Sugars Starch
Fat	Formed from fatty acids.	Energy production (+ tissue formation) Excess stored in fatty deposits and liver	Oils, fats
Minerals	Chemical ions	Regulate body processes	Iron - used in blood. Calcium - used in bone.
Vitamins	Complex compounds formed by plants	Regulate physiological processes eg by forming enzymes	Vitamins A, B, C, D etc.

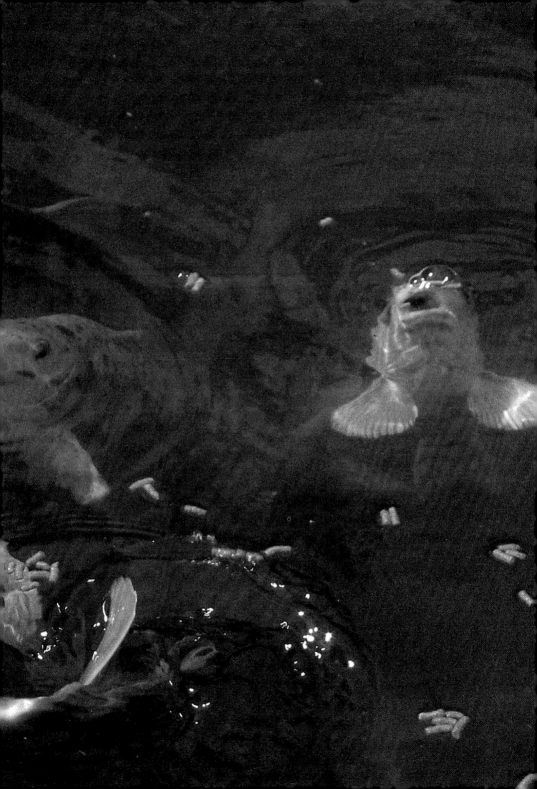

type of fish, maturity, etc. Before considering how the requirements change it will be useful to examine Table 1 which shows how these nutrients are used in the body of a koi. All of these nutrients are required throughout the life of the koi, but in greatly differing proportions. The protein requirements are perhaps the best example. Fry and young fish grow very rapidly in their first few years, often increasing in length by 10-20cm each year.

Proteins, or more correctly amino acids, are used for tissue formation and because they cannot be stored in the body, the koi fry and young need to obtain large quantities on a regular basis.

In the wild, young carp feed largely on zooplankton (eg daphnia and copepods) followed by benthic invertebrates (eg bloodworms and freshwater shrimps) which are both rich in protein. In captivity we should reproduce this by feeding a diet which has a relatively high protein content. Research has shown that koi fry require a diet containing 45% protein and young fish require a lower protein concentration in the food of approximately 30%.

This general reduction in the amount of protein required by the koi as they grow is complicated by seasonal variations and the reproductive cycle. In the winter when water temperatures in the koi pond fall below 15°C the koi will only grow very slowly "if at all" and should be given a relatively low protein food. Above 15°C the koi will grow rapidly and should be given a higher protein diet. At these higher temperatures even mature koi, which are not growing rapidly will require a high protein diet to form reproductive tissues or to repair damaged tissues.

What to Feed

There are a number of commercially available foods which have been specially formulated for koi. These foods vary considerably in terms of their quality and the nutrients contained in them. It is important to choose a proven make of food to ensure that your fish receive all of the nutrients that they require. This is particularly so with koi, which are often kept in a relatively bare pond, with few other sources of food available.

Commercial foods such as those in the Tetra range are available in powder, flake and stick forms and the choice depends largely on what the fish can fit in their mouths. As a guide fry up to 2cm in length should be given a powdered food (such as Tetra Baby Fish Food for Egglayers); those between 2 and 6cm should be fed on flaked foods (eg Tetra Growth Food and TetraFin Goldfish Flake); whilst larger indi-

page 38/39: The fish in your pond should rise eagerly to the surface at each feed. If they do not you may be overfeeding. (Wieser).

Food from the TetraPond range provides a balanced nutritional diet for your koi throughout the year.

viduals should be given a stick food. Larger fish will still feed on flaked foods, but tend to ignore small particles which will remain uneaten and can pollute the water.

Tetra stick foods come in a range of formulations to provide your koi with their exact nutritional requirements throughout the year. At low temperatures koi will not feed actively and their digestive systems do not function efficiently. Below 12°C therefore, they should be given a maintenance food which has a high carbohydrate and low protein level. Little growth occurs at these temperatures therefore protein will not be utilised and could pollute the water. TetraPond Floating Foodsticks provide the ideal diet under these conditions. As the temperature rises some growth occurs, therefore the fish should also be offered a slightly higher protein food which still has all of the other nutrients required for a balanced diet. At these temperatures both TetraPond Floating Foodsticks and TetraPond Koi Sticks should be used. Finally, above 16°C the koi will be growing rapidly and require a higher protein diet. In the wild carp obtain this through the increased numbers of insect larvae present in the summer. In a koi pond it can be provided in the form of TetraPond Growth Food for Koi. This food has a protein level of 42% and includes all of the amino acids the koi require for rapid growth. At high temperatures the Growth Food for Koi may be used on its own or in combination with Tetra Koi and Floating Foodsticks.

Additional Foods

Although the Tetra range of koi foods will provide your fish with all of their nutritional needs, every koi keeper likes to give their fish an occasional treat. Earthworms, silkworm pupae and small quantities of brown bread can all be used as a koi treat. In addition koi are particularly fond of fresh plant material - which is rich in vitamin C.

In most ponds there will be some plants or blanketweed and any new growth will be eagerly eaten. Alternatively whole lettuces, watercress or even orange segments will be appreciated. Whole lettuces are

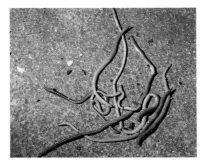

Earthworms are an ideal treat food for larger koi. They are also useful to tempt the appetite of unhealthy fish.

particularly liked by large koi, and if added in the evening, will often be shredded or have disappeared completely by the following morning.

Colour Enhancing Foods

The colouration of all koi is determined by the relative amounts of three colour pigments (red, black and yellow) within the skin of the fish. So, for example, the orange colouration of some varieties is a result of red and yellow pigmentation, whereas brown is due to black and yellow. In addition there are reflective cells called irridocytes which produce the metallic sheen of some fish and can interfere with the colour produced by the above pigments. Blue, for example, is due to black pigment covered by irridocytes.

The colour pigments are contained within the chromatophores, the density and distribution of which is determined genetically. The fish themselves cannot manufacture

colour pigments and need to consume them as part of their diet. In the wild naturally occurring colour enhancers are found in certain algae, plants and invertebrates (eg shrimps). In the pond or aquarium it is very unlikely that there will be sufficient naturally occurring colour enhancers to satisfy the needs of all of the fish. Therefore commercially available foods such as TetraPond Koi Sticks, which contain these natural colour enhancers, should be given on a regular basis. In this way the full colour potential of the fish will be realised.

What Not to Feed

Many koi keepers give their koi a range of foods which are unsuitable particularly if given in large quantities. White bread, trout pellets, sweetcorn and potatoes are examples of feeds which should not be given in large quantities as they will result in the fish becoming very overweight. Dyed maggots should also be avoided as there is evidence to suggest that some of the dyes (ie chrysodine - a bronze dye) may cause cancers.

How Much and When to Feed

The amount of food to give to a koi depends on numerous factors including temperature and the size of the fish. We have already discussed how the protein requirement varies as the fish grows. This is also true of the quantity of food required for healthy growth as is shown in Table

2. In general as the fish grows its metabolism slows down and consequently its food requirements are reduced.

Anyone who keeps koi or other coldwater fish will be aware that they consume less food as the temperature decreases. This is due to fish being coldblooded. As their body temperature decreases so does their metabolic rate which, as already discussed, results in them consuming less food.

Koi will continue feeding even at a temperature of 4°C, although the quantities of food consumed at the lower temperature is very small. In fact it is advisable to follow the of-

Avoid feeding live food captured in the wild. The copepod (above left) contains four larval tapeworms which, if eaten by a small koi, would develop into Bothriocephalus acheilognathi - the Chinese tapeworm of carp .

White bread should only be given as an occasional treat food as it can lead to the koi becoming too fat.

ten quoted rule and not feed the fish when the temperature falls below 8°C. It is not that the koi will not feed below this temperature but they will be able to obtain what little nutrition they require from within the pond (eg from algae) or from their energy reserves. If you feed at temperatures below 8°C there is a good chance that some food will be uneaten and will subsequently pollute the water.

TABLE 2

QUANTITY OF DRIED FOOD REQUIRED EACH DAY TO ENCOURAGE RAPID GROWTH OF KOI

Fish Size	Amount of Food Required per day (as a percentage of body weight)
Newly hatched fry (less than 2cm long)	15 - 20%
Older fry (3g in weight, 2 - 4cm long)	10 - 15%
10g in weight approximately 5cm long	5%
100g in weight approximately 12cm long	2%

Additionally, if the temperature falls still further after feeding, some of the food may remain in the intestine for a long period of time and lead to intestinal disorders such as ulceration (caused by the acidic digestive secretions remaining in contact with the intestine for a prolonged period of time). On occasions throughout the winter there are times when the water temperature rises slightly and the fish begin to actively search for food. At these times very small quantities of cereal based foods or earthworms may be given. Earthworms are particularly good as they are over 90% water, making it difficult for the fish to overfeed, and if not eaten they can easily be removed. Throughout the warmer months (water temperature above 10°C) the koi should be fed 2-4 times each day on as much food as they will consume within 5 minutes. By following this rule, you will automatically alter the feeding in accordance with the changing water temperature throughout the summer.

With care koi can be trained to accept food form your hands.

When the fish are feeding actively the time of feeding is unimportant. There is no truth in the idea that koi should not be fed in the early morning or evening - after all that is precisely when wild carp are feeding most actively.

Pond Additives

Not all of a koi's nutrient requirements are obtained from its food. In fact many vitamins and minerals can be absorbed across the gill membrane. The algae which form "green water" provide one example of this. They release a number of vitamins into the water which improve the colouration and overall health of the koi. Anyone catching koi or goldfish from a pond which has been "green" throughout the summer will certainly notice this. These vitamins are present in Tetra Koi Vital, a pond additive which allows you to have the benefits of "green water" with none of the disadvantages. The importance of fish nutrition and providing a balanced diet cannot be overstated. A good quality food in the correct quantities will help to ensure your fish remain in good condition and grow rapidly.

Healthy koi and clear water should be the aim of every koi keeper.

KOI HEALTH

Koi, in common with all of the fish we keep in ponds or aquaria, are subject to a range of different ailments. In the past our knowledge of these diseases and why they occurred was limited, with the result that many koi died (and they were consequently regarded as difficult fish to keep). In recent years, however, our understanding of the needs of the koi has increased greatly and losses should now be the exception rather than the rule.

How do Koi Become Diseased?

Before looking at the diseases which can affect koi, it is important to point out that all of the koi that you keep, and for that matter all of those that are for sale, are diseased. That is they are all infected by at least one, and often several, species of parasites. Those parasites are a natural part of the environment of the koi.

If the koi is in good condition generally, its immune system (the body's natural means of countering disease) will be active and capable of controlling the infection, ensuring that the parasites are only present in very small numbers. Exactly the same is true in humans. Each of us are infected by a number of different species of disease organisms, such as cold viruses, flu viruses, and perhaps something considerably more serious. But if we are other-

Even apparently healthy koi such as this Yamabuki Hariwake have small numbers of parasites on them.

wise healthy, our immune system will naturally control these diseases and we will feel healthy. If the koi becomes unhealthy for any reason, for example due to poor water quality, unsuitable nutrition or stress, the immune system will be suppressed, allowing the existing parasites to increase in numbers and cause problems.

A second situation when disease is likely to occur is following the introduction of new fish into the aquarium or pond. Although these fish may appear perfectly healthy they will, as already indicated, harbour small numbers of parasites. If the species (or even the strain) of parasite is "new" to the koi already in your pond, their immune system will not recognise the organism as being harmful and will initially not control it. As a result the parasites may increase to dangerous numbers causing the koi to become unhealthy.

Disease Diagnosis

For effective disease control it is essential that diseases are diagnosed at an early stage and correct treatment is administered. The first stage of this diagnosis is actually recognising that a fish is unhealthy.

Recognising ill-health is relatively easy, particularly for the koi keeper. This is because most koi keepers feed their fish several times a day and quickly learn to recognise the normal colouration and behaviour of each individual.

If a fish looks or behaves differently it is a sign that something has changed (not necessarily for the worst!) and should be investigated further. Signs which may indicate poor health include:

Gasping	Rubbing
Rapid breathing	Listlessness
Change in colour	Emaciation
Obvious parasites	'Slimy' appearance
Spending much time away from the other fish	Not eating

If these signs are observed it is important to have a closer look at the fish concerned in order to determine the cause. It may not be ill-health, for example, in cool weather the intensity of colour in a koi will improve, or when salt is added the colour will fade. Both examples are not problems but are worth checking.

The secret when deciding what has affected your koi is not to jump to conclusions. Decide firstly why the fish is behaving as it is and then what would cause it to do so. The possible causes can then be examined to determine the actual cause.

For example, a koi is seen to be gasping at the water surface. The fish is gasping because it cannot get sufficient oxygen (there is more oxygen in the water at the surface). This may be due to a lack of oxygen in the water, raised pollutant levels, excess chlorine or pesticides, gill parasites or blood parasites. If there are raised pollutant levels, chlorine or pesticides in the water, the gills may be damaged which will reduce their efficiency, or excess mucus may be produced as a protective mechanism by the fish, but which coats the gills and reduces oxygen uptake. Gill parasites would have the same effect - gill damage and excess mucus production. Blood parasites would absorb oxygen from the blood so preventing it reaching the vital organs. As you can see, there are many explanations for a fish gasping. If you immediately assume gasping is due to too little oxygen in the water you may lose your fish due to a gill parasite infection.

As a second example let us look at a fish which is rubbing against the pond sides. Taking the problem step by step we should have:

Signs of bad health:	Scratching
Reason for behaviour:	Irritation of the skin or gills
Causes:	Poor water quality (raised ammonia nitrite, nitrate, chlorine, pesticides, remedies, etc, altered pH). Gill parasites, Skin parasites.

A further cause of rubbing which is worth noting is the presence of particles in the water which get caught on the gill tissue. This often occurs following feeding. Koi chew their food using throat teeth and particles which become trapped are removed by back-flushing the gills or by rubbing. This behaviour can often be seen for a few minutes after each feed and is no cause for concern.

The next stage in diagnosis is to decide which of the possible causes is responsible for the poor health in your fish. One clue to the cause can be found in the time of onset and the rate of spread. There are three main possibilities.

1. Only one or two fish are affected and the problem does not spread to any other fish. This suggests a non-infectious disease (ie the life cycle cannot be completed in the pond or aquarium) or a malformation.

2. A small number of fish are affected initially, but this number gradually increases over a period of days or weeks. This suggests an infectious disease.

3. All the fish in the pond are affected or all of the fish of the same species or size, and the disease occurs rapidly (say overnight). This suggests a water quality problem.

If you suspect an infectious or non-infectious disease a more accurate diagnosis can be obtained by carefully examining the fish for signs of disease and/or damage. This can be achieved in a pond but is better if the affected fish is placed in a polythene bag where it can be viewed from the side and underneath.

"The Tetra Manual of Fish Health" by Dr C Andrews, A Excell and N Carrington, published by Tetra and ADI No 49 - "Water Chemistry and Fish Diseases", published by Tetra provide a good illustrated guide to fish parasites.

Water Quality

If poor water quality if suspected it is important to locate the cause of the problem and correct it. Events prior to your fish becoming unhealthy often provide vital clues to its cause. If you suspect poor water quality, did the signs of poor health occur immediately after the addition of tapwater? (suggesting chlorine or a sudden pH change could be responsible); after the addition of new fish or cleaning the filter? (suggesting raised ammonia or nitrate levels); or following recent treatment? (suggesting overdosing, mixing remedies or the filter being adversely affected).

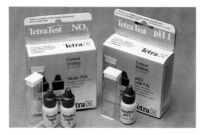

Poor water quality can be detected before it adversely affects the koi using good quality test kits.

Careful testing of the water quality will often enable you to detect the cause of the problem. The water should, for example, be tested for pollutants using Tetra Ammonia and Nitrite Test Kits. Raised levels of these pollutants may be dangerous to the fish and indicate that the filter is not functioning effectively, the pond is overstocked, there is excess debris or uneaten food in the water, or perhaps an unseen, dead fish is present. High pH levels can be a problem, particularly where there is unsealed cement in or around the pond. This can be quickly detected using a Tetra pH Test Kit. Nearby spraying using pesticides can also

affect the pond and not be detected using the available test kits.

When poor water quality is detected a large (30-50%) partial water change will immediately dilute the problem (providing it is not in the tapwater). The replacement water should be a similar temperature to that in the pond and be de-chlorinated using TetraPond AquaFin. The cause of the problem should then be located and corrected.

COMMON DISEASES OF KOI

Whitespot
(Ichthyophthirius multifilis)
SIGNS: Small pinhead sized white spots on the skin and fins. Cause severe irritation to the fish, which will rub against underwater objects and clamp their fins against their body. Do not confuse with pale breeding tubercles which occur on the head and pectoral fins of male koi, goldfish, orfe, etc, at breeding time.
TREATMENT: Whitespot can spread very rapidly from fish to fish,

Pinhead white spots are typical of the disease white spot.

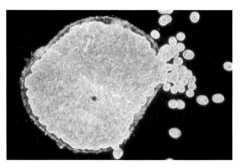

The white spot parasite drops off the fish to complete its life cycle. Each cyst gives rise to several hundred offspring

therefore prompt treatment is vital. The parasite drops off the fish to multiply, therefore the pond must always be treated. TetraPond DesaFin (= MediFin in the UK) will effectively control the whitespot parasite. In severe infections control may take 5-7 days.

Sliminess of the Skin

SIGNS: Fish become very irritated rubbing against underwater objects and jumping. In severe cases they swim in a listless fashion, with fins folded against their body and often isolated from other fish. Closer inspection may reveal a grey slimy coating over the body or in patches - particularly obvious against dark areas of the body and eyes. The irritation may be caused by poor water quality (raised levels of ammonia and nitrite, sudden pH change or excess chlorine in newly added tapwater), skin and gill parasites, eg protozoans (costia, chilodonella, whitespot) and flukes.

TREATMENT: If all fish are affected, check the water quality using Tetra Test Kits and correct as described earlier. Treat all new tapwater with TetraPond AquaFin. Treat the parasites in the pond with TetraPond DesaFin (= MediFin). The worst affected individuals may be isolated and treated with DesaFin or, in aquaria with Tetra Medica ContraSpot.

Fungus

SIGNS: Cottonwool like growths on the body or fins of the fish. Usually white, but may trap algae or debris and appear green or brown.

TREATMENT: TetraPond DesaFin (= MediFin) added to the pond will control fungus infections. Alternatively, the affected fish may be isolated and treated using DesaFin or, in aquaria, using Tetra Medica FungiStop. Fungi only attack fish that have been weakened in some way. Infections are particularly common

Under the microscope fungus resembles tiny thread like strands

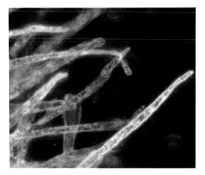

in the spring, after spawning and following bad handling.

Fin Rot

SIGNS: The fins and tail appear to be eaten away from the outer edge. In severe cases reddening may occur at the base of the fins and surrounding muscles.

Fin rot is caused by the opportunistic bacteria which eat the fin membranes.

TREATMENT: TetraPond DesaFin (= MediFin) added to the pond will treat the bacteria responsible for fin rot. Alternatively isolate the fish and treat with TetraMedica General Tonic. The damaged fins will regenerate. Fin rot only attacks fish that are weakened, usually through poor water quality or physical damage. It is therefore important to improve pond conditions by conducting a partial water change and removing excess debris. Also avoid damaging the fish when handling.

Fish Pox

SIGNS: White, pink or grey growths on the skin and fins, resembling drops of molten wax. Usually relatively hard to the touch. Fish pox is

Fish pox on the dorsal fin of a Koi. (Photograph courtesy of J. Chubb)

a viral infection which is common on koi, although gold-fish, orfe and rudd are also susceptible. Although fish pox is unsightly it is not dangerous and rarely, if ever, does any harm to the fish.

TREATMENT: There is no reliable treatment for fish pox. Improving the overall condition of the fish (by improving pond hygiene, raising the water temperature, and providing a balanced diet) will stimulate the fish's immune system. which may overcome the disease. Very often the disease will occur in the spring, only to disappear as the water temperature rises.

Ulceration

SIGNS: Reddened sores on the body of the fish. Usually caused by the removal of a scale or physical damage which becomes infected with bacteria and enlarges. Often the fish will appear unaffected and will continue to feed.

TREATMENT: In the early stages ulcers may be controlled by isolating the fish and treating with Tetra Pond DesaFin (= MediFin) or Tetra

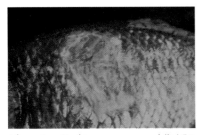

Ulceration "in this case on a goldfish" is due to a bacterial infection of a wound. (photograph courtesy of J. Chubb)

Medica General Tonic. If the ulcer appears inflamed the fish may be removed from the water and full strength General Tonic carefully painted onto the wound. Keep the concentrated General Tonic away from the gills and eyes, and do not use on ulcers on or close to the head. To prevent the remedy washing away, the wound may be covered with a setting agent such as "Orabase", Vaseline or Friars Balsam. This treatment should be repeated at 2 day intervals until the ulcer begins to heal. The fish should also be placed in a container in which 1 ounce of cooking salt is added to every gallon of water. This will prevent water passing into the body of the fish through the wound. More severe ulceration should be treated with antibiotics (obtained from a vet in the UK). If the fish is still feeding, oxalinic acid medicated feed is usually effective.

Fish Leech

SIGNS: Affected fish will become very irritated, rubbing against un-derwater objects and showing occasional quick bursts of swimming. Closer examination will reveal worm-like leeches up to 3cm in length. *Piscicola geometra*, the most common species, is an olive green colour with paler bands along the body. Many other leeches present in ponds are not parasitic.

TREATMENT: Remove the affected fish to a treatment container which has 15 level tablespoons of cooking salt per 10 litres of water (for 15-30 minutes). Those leeches which do not fall off can be easily pulled off using forceps. The fish may become reinfected when replaced in the pond. The leeches can be treated in the pond using organophosphorus based remedies available from aquatic stores (eg Naled and Masoten), but remove orfe and rudd before treatment and remove the leeches manually.

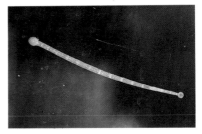

The fish leech (Piscicola geometra) can be identified by its olive green colour and paler rings. (Photograph: J. Chubb)

Fish Lice

SIGNS: Cause severe irritation to the affected fish and localised reddened areas often developing into ulceration. Close examination will reveal a disc-shaped parasite, up to 0.5cm in diameter. The fish will often show quick bursts of swimming and jumping out of the water.

A fish louse attached to the gill cover of a koi. (Photograph courtesy of J. Chubb)

TREATMENT: Organophosphorus based remedies are very effective, but are unsuitable for treating orfe and rudd. These fish should be removed and treated with one or two 30 minute baths in 0.1g potassium permanganate/10 litres of water. It is important to treat the entire pond, as the fish lice drop off the fish to digest their meals.

Gill Flukes

SIGNS: Irritation caused by the parasites will cause the fish to rub and jump, the fish may also gasp at the water surface and show rapid gill movements. In severe cases the fish will swim rapidly, rubbing occasionally, followed by periods of inactivity and rapid gill movements.
TREATMENT: TetraPond DesaFin (= MediFin) added to the pond will quickly control the gill flukes. In severe cases organophosphorus based remedies may also be used.

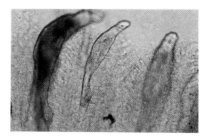

Gill flukes (Dactylogyrus vastator) attached to the gill filaments of a koi.

The effects of the parasites will be exaggerated by poor water conditions, therefore a partial water change and removing debris will help.

Gill Rot

SIGNS: Affected fish will become very lethargic, hanging near the water surface usually in the most oxygenated areas. The gills may be very red and swollen, occasionally protruding from the gill covers. Closer examination will reveal excess mucus production, pale or brown areas on the gill filaments and sometimes bleeding. Gill rot is caused by secondary bacterial infection or attack by a fungus called *Branchiomyces*.
TREATMENT: In many cases when the disease is diagnosed the fish is already too badly damaged for treatment to be successful. Mild salt dips (1.5 - 2.0 ounces per gallon) for 5 - 10 minutes daily and keeping the fish in water treated with Tetra-Medica General Tonic will help relieve gill inflammation and remove excess mucus without further dam-

aging the fish. If the fish survives, treatment with antibiotics or TetraPond DesaFin (= MediFin) may be used.

Treatment

The successful treatment of a fish disease relies largely on the early and accurate diagnosis of the parasite responsible. Once the parasite has been identified it is a relatively simple matter to select the correct remedy and administer it in a way in which it is likely to be successful. There are several methods of administering a disease remedy. These include:

1. Immersion
2. Topical Treatment
3. Injection
4. Stomach Tube
5. Medicated Food

1. Immersion

Adding the remedy to the aquarium or pond in which the diseased fish is swimming is the most widely used form of treatment. The vast majority of external parasites can safely be treated, with no adverse effects on the fish, by using a good quality remedy.

It is important to follow a few basic rules, if the remedy is to be effective:

a) Undertake a partial water change and remove any debris from the aquarium, pond and filter, prior to treatment. By doing so there will be little debris present to absorb the remedy.
b) Remove any chemical filter media, which will absorb the remedy (eg charcoal, zeolite).
c) Use the correct dosage - overdosing may damage weakened fish, while under dosing can lead to the parasites gaining immunity to the remedy.
d) Leave the remedy in the aquarium or pond for the prescribed time.
e) Follow any instructions that are provided with the remedy.
f) Do not mix remedies, unless the instructions say it is safe to do so.

2. Topical Treatment

Topical treatment involves applying a strong solution of an antiseptic or remedy directly onto the affected area of a fish. Cysts and ulcers are often treated in this way with the remedy being applied using a soft paintbrush or cottonwool bud. Suitable remedies include a full strength solution of a bacterial treatment, eg TetraMedica General Tonic (on ulcers), and a 0.1% solution of Mercurochrome (on cysts). Avoid touching the eyes and gills with these strong solutions as they can cause serious damage. Topical treatment should be repeated at 1-2 day intervals until the problem has disappeared.

3. Injection

Injections should only be carried out by trained, qualified personnel and are only applicable for large, easily handled fish. Antibiotics are the

Dropsy, in this case caused by an internal bacterial infection results in the body becoming greatly swollen.

usual remedy administered by injection in order to control internal bacterial infections or serious ulceration. Before injection, the fish should be anaesthetised using MS222 or Benzocaine to prevent it struggling and damaging itself. Suitable antibiotics should be obtained from a vet, who will provide an injectable form, together with the necessary dosage instructions. Antibiotics need to be injected 2 or 3 times over a week to 10 day period to ensure the fish are completely cured.

4. Stomach Tube

A stomach tube enables a remedy (usually an antibiotic) to be released into the intestine of the fish. As with injections, stomach tubing should only be undertaken by competent personnel to avoid damaging the fish. Anaesthetising is necessary, both to prevent the fish from struggling and to relax the throat musculature and allow the tube to pass into the intestine. A suitable tube can be made from a dog catheter (obtaina-

ble from a vet) together with a 10ml syringe.

5. Medicated Feed

This involves feeding the fish the required remedy mixed with a food. In theory this provides an ideal form of medication as it does not stress the fish. In practice one of the first signs of poor health in a fish is its reluctance to feed, therefore it will not oblige by eating the remedy. Consequently early disease diagnosis is essential so that treatment can start while the fish are still feeding. Antibiotics are the usual remedy administered in this way although anthelmintics (for worm infections) can also be used. Antibiotic medicated feeds such as Tetra Medicated Food are widely available in the US but have to be obtained through a vet in the UK. Alternatively medicated foods can be made at home:

a) By injecting the antibiotic into a favourite food such as an earthworm, prawn or piece of meat.

b) By forming a slurry of antibiotic and cooking oil or water, and mixing this with a small quantity of foods. The coated foods should be left to dry for 24-48 hours before use.

Medicated feeds need to be fed at daily intervals over a period of ten days. Dose rates vary depending on the antibiotic in question, but your vet will provide details.

c) A medicated tablet food is ideal for treating smaller fish (less than 4") and may be formed using tablets which can be stuck onto the aquarium glass (Tetra FD Tips are ideal). 5 or 6 of these tablets should be ground into a powder and mixed with the powdered remedy required to treat 1-10 fish for 10 days. The powder should be mixed with a little water, to form a stiff paste and applied to the outer surface of 10 tablets. The inner flat surface of the tablets should not be covered so that they can still be stuck to the glass. The coated tablets should be left to dry for 24 hours and used at the rate of 1 per day for the 10 day course of treatment.

Like humans, fish possess a very good immune system which can attack and control any disease organisms providing the fish is otherwise in good condition. Whatever treatment method is selected it is important that you encourage the fish's immune system so that it will also counter the disease.

The immune system of a fish is greatly affected by water temperature, being more active at higher temperatures and not active below 12°C (54°F). Before treating a fish

it is therefore advisable so slowly raise the water temperature (2°C per day) to above 12°C and preferably to above 15°C. If the pond temperature is already above 15°C, raising it a further 2-3°C will stimulate the immune system. A partial water change prior to treatment is also advisable as this will often improve the water quality to the benefit of the fish. Good water quality should always be maintained throughout the treatment period. Finally it is important to keep the fish feeding. If necessary, this can be achieved using "safe" live foods such as bloodworms or earthworms.

Disease Prevention

With a little care, the diseases described in this section can be prevented allowing your koi to remain in the best possible condition. In fact the prevention of disease should be the aim of every koi keeper and is more satisfactory than trying to treat a disease outbreak once it has occurred.

Most, if not all, of the koi in your pond will have disease organisms on them, but, as mentioned earlier the koi's immune system will control the parasites if the fish is otherwise healthy. Good koi keeping, that is maintaining good water quality, using the correct food, avoiding overstocking etc. is therefore the best way of preventing the fish becoming weakened and susceptible to disease. The introduction of new fish into a pond can result in the intro-

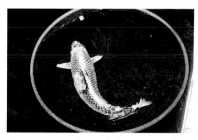

Even severe physical damage such as this wound can heal quickly if the koi are kept in good conditions.

duction of new parasites. If the species (or even the strain) of parasite is "new" to the existing koi their immune system will not recognise the parasite as harmful and will initially not control it. As a result the parasites may increase to dangerous levels causing the koi to become unhealthy. Choosing healthy koi (see section on buying koi) and taking precautions before introducing them into your pond will help to minimise this risk.

Quarantine

Quarantining all new fish is important in order to avoid the introduction of disease into your aquarium or pond. The quarantine period, which should ideally last for 3 to 4 weeks, will allow you to observe the koi for signs of disease which may become apparent following the stress of transportation; enable the koi to acclimatise to the water conditions in your area; allow the koi to settle down before being introduced into a new pond; and enable you to treat any new disease outbreaks. It is important, however, that the quarantine container is suitable, otherwise the health of the koi may be adversely affected.

The Quarantine Container

The container used for quarantining you koi need not be over elaborate, but must be large enough to support the koi and maintain good water quality. A second pond in your garden or garage is the ideal quarantine container, but may be impractical for many koi keepers. The pool will double as a treatment container for any unhealthy fish and so would be a useful investment for anyone with a large koi collection. Temporary quarantine (and treatment) containers are more popular. These can be in the form of a PVC holding pond (such as the ones used for koi shows), a child's paddling pool or a DIY construction. A temporary pool can, for example, be made using straw bales or a wooden frame and a polythene liner.

As far as size is concerned you should allow at least 900cm of water surface area for every 2.5cm of fish length. Therefore for a 25cm (10 inch) koi you would need a surface area of 9000cm (10 square feet). The depth should be at least 45cm. The quarantine pond should be positioned out of direct sunlight and away from chilling winds and frost in order to avoid sudden and potentially dangerous changes in water temperature.

Water Quality

Filtration for the quarantine container is important in order to maintain good water quality. The filter and pump should be large enough to turn over the pool volume every hour. Raised levels of ammonia and nitrite often occur in the quarantine container when new fish are introduced due to the filter not being mature. This can be prevented by keeping the filter running continually and having a hardy koi or goldfish in the pond. This fish will also pacify newly introduced fish and result in them settling down more quickly. Chemical filter media (eg Zeolite) are useful as they work instantly and will help to prevent raised ammonia and nitrite levels. Remember to remove the chemical media if any remedies are added. Regular partial water changes and the removal of any debris will also help to maintain good water quality. It is important to check the water using Tetra Test Ammonia and Nitrite test kits in order to detect and correct any water quality problems before they adversely affect the koi. Daily testing is advisable in the first 7 to 10 days after adding the fish, followed by tests every 2 to 3 days until the fish are released into your main pond.

Koi Behaviour

Newly introduced koi will be nervous in the confines of the quarantine container, particularly if other fish are not present. It is therefore wise to cover the pool with a net to prevent the koi from jumping out. In addition you should provide some form of shelter, eg. a plastic bucket turned on its side and ensure that there are areas of slow water flow.

Disease Treatment

During the quarantine period it is advisable to treat the koi with a general external parasite remedy such as TetraPond MediFin in order to remove any external parasites. Any obvious parasites should be treated as described previously.

Feeding

The koi should be fed throughout the quarantine period, although in some cases it may be necessary to use "safe" live foods such as earthworms in order to tempt newly introduced fish to feed. Avoid overfeeding the koi.

Alternatives to Quarantine

If you do not have a quarantine container there is a greater risk of introducing diseases into your pond. Before purchasing koi in these circumstances it is wise to ask your dealer how long the fish have been in stock. If the koi have been at the dealers for several weeks and appear healthy there should be little risk. However, it is worth treating the fish with a general parasite remedy before introduction. This can be achieved by either treating the entire pond, or using a short term dip. These measures may seem excessive when you buy apparently healthy koi from your dealer. However, following the stress of capture, handling and transportation, the koi can become diseased and this disease may well spread to the other fish in your collection. Quarantining all new fish is far easier and safer than attempting to treat a disease outbreak in your koi pond.

BREEDING KOI

Koi can be successfully bred in any well kept koi pool or garden pond. This not only indicates that conditions in the pond are ideal and the fish healthy but also provides a further area of interest for the koi keeper.

In many cases the koi spawn naturally and the first indication the hobbyist has is the vigorous chasing of the spawning fish, or the presence of small fish sometime after the event. Such spawnings can produce healthy fry although they are generally of poor quality in terms of pattern and colouration. The numbers of fry surviving will also be low due to the other fish in the pond consuming both the eggs and young fish. The success of these random spawnings can be greatly improved by adopting some of the suggestions outlined in this section. For the more adventurous koi keeper it is also possible to select the parents with, for example, desirable colouration, pattern or size in order to produce high quality offspring.

Where to Breed the Fish

Before attempting to breed your koi some consideration must be given to where they are going to spawn. There are a number of options open to the koi keeper:

1. **Random Spawning:** The most simple option is to allow the koi to breed in the pond. The eggs will be deposited on any plants or blanketweed in the pond or along the sides. Large numbers of eggs and fry will be consumed by the parents, but it is possible to save some. The eggs should be moved via the plants or algae to which they are attached and placed in a container filled with pond water. In this way they will not be physically damaged or subject to any sudden changes in water quality.

2. **Spawning Media:** To increase the numbers of eggs which are saved you can add a spawning

Spawning ropes can be placed in your koi pool and removed to a rearing container when covered in eggs. (photograph courtesy of R. Cleaver)

medium to the pond before the koi breed and remove it together with the eggs afterwards. Hornwort or water hyacinth make ideal natural materials or you could use the artificial spawning ropes which are available commercially.

3. **Koi Spawning Nets:** Perhaps the most popular way of spawning selected fish is to use a spawning net. These nets are constructed in a box shape from very soft fine mesh. The usual dimensions range from 1.2 x 1.2 x 0.5m up to 1.2 x 4.0 x 1.0m. The net is supported in the koi pond by means of floats or a framework of pipes. Ideally the net should extend 10-20cm above the water surface to prevent the fish jumping out in the excitement of spawning. Spawning nets allow the selected parents to be isolated from the rest of the pond whilst still benefitting from your existing filtration system. A further advantage is that the nets are very soft and so minimise any damage which could occur during spawning.

4. **Separate Pond:** Few koi keepers are fortunate to have a separate pond which can be used for breeding purposes.

However, an adequate temporary pool can be constructed at low cost using heavy duty polythene or a pond liner supported using bricks,

A spawning net suspended in the pond helps to minimise damage during spawning and provides a good nursery for eggs or fry.
(Photograph courtesy of R.Cleaver)

wood or even bales of straw. Remember that you may need filtration to keep the water quality in good condition.

Selecting the Parents

If you intend to breed from selected parents it is advisable to use two or three males to every female as this ensures a better fertility rate.

Koi are very difficult to sex when they are less than 25cm in length because they are immature. Above this size it can still be difficult until the fish are in spawning condition. Male koi generally have a more slender shape and a more pointed head in relation to the rest of the body. The leading edge of the pectoral fins is usually thicker than in the females. The distance from the front of the head to the pectoral fins is usually greater in a male koi, and these fins are larger in proportion to the rest of the body. When in breeding condition the abdomen of the female becomes swollen and is softer than the males. The vent of the female at this stage is large and flat whereas in the male it is smaller, more elongate and concave. In addition the male develops small, pale raised breeding tubercles on the head and leading edge of the pectoral fin. These are often difficult to see but give the fish a rough texture when handled.

Whichever parent fish you select to breed, the offspring will always be a mixture of varieties. This is even true if you use high quality, line bred specimens, although here the proportion of fry of the same type will be very much greater. In general, if you want to produce large numbers of fry of a given variety, you should use parents of that variety. So, for example, using Kohakus as parents will give large numbers of Kohaku fry.

Conditioning the Koi

Before your fish spawn it is advisable to get them in the best possible condition to overcome the rigours of breeding and to allow healthy ovary and testes development. To do this the koi should be fed in the normal way in the spring, with a low protein diet being offered as soon as the water temperature is above 8°C. At a water temperature of 15°C and above, a high protein diet food such as TetraPond Growth Food for Koi should be offered several times a day. The protein in this food will be used to form the reproductive organs.

Spawning Behaviour

Koi, in common with other coldwater fish, tend to spawn in late spring and summer when the water temperatures rise to 20°C. The rise in water temperature combined with sunlight acts as a stimulus to the spawning. The first sign of the impending spawning is the males chasing the females and nudging their abdomens. This behaviour often starts in the evening or early morning. The chasing behaviour

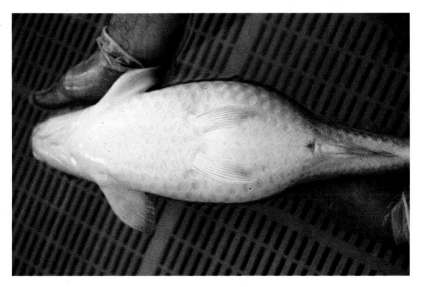

A female koi immediately before spawning - note the bloated appearance caused by the fully developed eggs.
(Photograph courtesy of R.Cleaver)

A male koi, note the large pectoral fins and longer, thinner head.
(Photograph courtesy of R.Cleaver)

The breeding behavior of koi is very active resulting in the fish forcing their way into the shallows or areas of dense plant growth.

increases in intensity until the males drive the female into the spawning medium. Here she releases the eggs and they are immediately fertilised by the male. The adhesive eggs are approximately 2mm in diameter and stick to the spawning medium as well as other objects in the vicinity. Around 100,000 eggs are produced for every kilogram of body weight, therefore a large female may produce up to half a million eggs.

If the parents will not spawn despite conditions being apparently favourable, it is often possible to stimulate spawning by changing part of the water, moving the net or temporary container to a more sunny position, or by separating the parents for 1-2 days. A rise in the water temperature of 4-5°C often stimulates

breeding but is not practical in most ponds.

Raising the Fry

The eggs will hatch after 2-7 days depending on the water temperature with them taking longer in cooler water. The ideal temperature is from 20-23°C. Avoid extreme values (below 17°C or above 25°C) as fewer eggs will hatch and more of

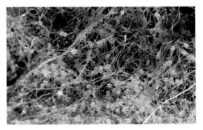

The result of successful spawning, koi eggs on blanket weed.

the fry will be deformed. The addition of a fungus treatment such as Tetra Medica FungiStop is advisable to prevent live eggs being infected.

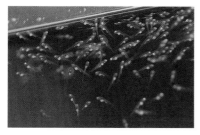

Koi fry shortly after hatching, measuring approximately 7mm in length.

Immediately after hatching the fry cling to any plants or algae by means of an adhesive pad on their heads.

At this stage the fry feed on their yolk sacs and so do not need any additional food. 2-3 days later the fry become more active and immediately swim up to the surface and take several gulps of air which are swallowed and forced into the swimbladder.

This added buoyancy allows the fry to swim more freely and begin to actively search for food. In the pond this is present in the form of microscopic animals. In an aquarium or other similar rearing container mature pond water should be added several times a day. After 1-2 days the fry will readily accept Tetra Baby Fish Food for Egglayers. This may be given 3-5 times each day but take care not to overfeed and pollute the water.

In the rearing container or aquarium, regular partial water changes and efficient filtration are essential in order to maintain good water quality. Foam filters (eg Tetra Brillant) are more suitable for the fry container than are undergravel or power filters, because they are easy to maintain and will not suck up the fry. Partial water changes should be conducted at 3-4 day intervals initially. On each occasion remove any excess debris that has accumulated. The replacement water must be the same temperature as that in the container and be de-chlorinated using TetraPond AquaFin or Tetra AquaSafe. Good aeration is important in the container to ensure that the water is oxygenated which is essential for the fry. Regular water quality tests are advisable to allow you to detect and correct problems before they adversely affect the fry.

Fry Selection and Growing on

Given good water conditions and food, the fry will grow rapidly. The maximum growth you could expect given ideal conditions is as follows:

Age	Length (cm)
30 days	1.5 - 2.0
60 days	2.5 - 3.0
6 months	16.0 - 18.0
1 year	18.0 - 23.0
2 years	23.0 - 30.0
3 years	30.0 - 35.0

The fry will grow at greatly different rates with the larger fry always getting to the food first and getting even bigger.

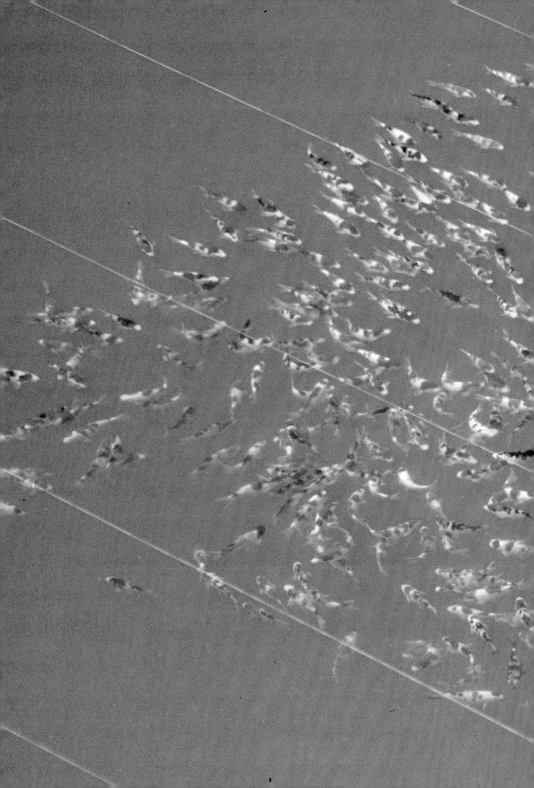

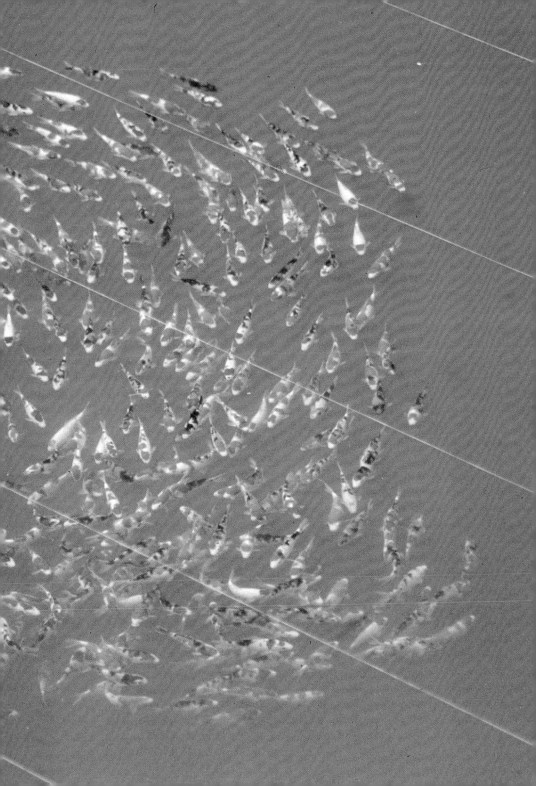

These large fry may become cannibalistic and consume the smaller individuals. In most cases it is the small fry which have the desirable characteristics and therefore need protecting.

Ensure that the fry do not become overcrowded in the rearing container as they grow. This can lead to water quality problems and retard development. If you aim to keep the stocking rate at a maximum of 2.5cm (1 inch) of fry for every 150cm2 (24 square inches) of water surface the fish should grow rapidly.

Fry Selection

It is rarely possible to raise all of the fry that hatch from a single spawning, simply because of the space required to raise thousands of young fish.

It is therefore necessary to select the koi fry with desirable characteristics which are to be kept and give away or discard the remainder.

Japanese koi breeders cull the fry three times in the first year, in many cases reducing the numbers to only 0.12% of those which hatched. Therefore, in a typical koi farm, 5 million fry will hatch in June and in July this number will be reduced to 500,000 by careful selection. In August a second selection reduces the numbers to 50,000 and a third selection in September leaves only 6,000 fry to overwinter.

Knowing which koi to discard and which to keep is one of the skills which allows Japanese breeders to produce the best koi in the world. The hobbyist cannot expect to match the generations of expertise that are used by the koi breeders, but it is still possible to make certain selections. At the first selection, after 4-5 weeks, any fry with malformations or which are obviously not of the desired variety should be removed. If you intend to breed kohakus, for example, the first selection would remove fry with any black markings or individuals which are "throwbacks" to the wild form. At the second and third selection the fry are selected for desirable colourations, patterning, etc, which varies according to the variety of koi in question.

Further information on the desirable characteristics of each variety of koi and therefore what you should select for amongst your fry is available in texts on koi varieties such as, "The Tetra Encyclopedia of Koi", published by Tetra and "Modern Nishikigoi" by Takeo Kuroki.

page 66/67: Koi fry in a japanese breeding pond. note the fine wires positioned above the water surface to prevent predation by fish eating birds.

POND MAINTENANCE

Regular maintenance of your pond and filter is very important if your pond is to remain attractive and the fish within it in the best possible condition. Many of the maintenance tasks will be covered in the next section on seasonal care of your fish, but several areas need to be considered in more depth.

Cleaning the Pond

Regular cleaning of the pond will help to keep ideal water conditions for your fish and should prevent the need for a complete clean out. The aim of the regular cleaning is to remove any debris which has accumulated on the pond bottom or sides which, if not removed, would be regularly disturbed by the digging activity of the koi and result in wa-

A pond vacuum being used to remove debris from the pond. (Photograph courtesy of R Cleaver).

ter cloudiness. In addition such debris would decompose and possibly pollute the pond water.

The filter will usually take out large amounts of debris, particularly if the inflow is positioned at the deepest point in the pond. Should any debris remain it can easily be removed by hand. Pond vacuum cleaners are available which are ideal for this purpose, such cleaners resemble household vacuums, with a powerful external pump being used to draw water and debris through a moveable length of pipe. This dirty water is disposed of into a waste drain. In carefully designed koi ponds, the water flows in a circular manner around the pond and in doing so concentrates any debris in the centre. This material may be easily removed by a pond vacuum. Alternatively a bottom drain or pump can be placed at this point to feed the filter.

Where such elaborate equipment is not available, the coarse debris can be removed using a fine net and the remaining material sucked up using the pond pump. If this method is adopted it is wise to discard the dirty water rather than feeding it into the filter, and also to clean the pump afterwards to avoid clogging or damage.

The frequency of pond cleaning depends largely on the amount of waste being produced. In the

summer it may be necessary at 1 or 2 day intervals, whereas, in the winter it should only be necessary every 3 to 4 weeks. In general if there is a build up of debris it should be removed.

Cleaning the Filter

The filter is the site at which material is mechanically removed from the water and biologically decomposed. This can result in the filter becoming blocked with debris which greatly reduces its efficiency. Regular cleaning, if done correctly will ensure that the filter works at maximum efficiency and helps to maintain perfect water quality. Mechanical filter media must be cleaned at regular intervals in order to remove the large particles of debris they have trapped. Removable mechanical media, eg foam or filter brushes can be taken out of the filter and washed in a strong jet of water. Settlement chambers and vortex units should be drained and the debris disturbed so that it can all be discarded. When cleaning these media make sure that the dirty water does not drain back into the pond or into the biological part of the filter. Biological filter media need to be cleaned more carefully to avoid losing the helpful filter bacteria. Large particles of debris should have been removed by the mechanical filter medium, but fine particles

and a bacterial mulm can become trapped within the biological filter. If this occurs the flow of oxygenated water to that section of the filter is reduced and the bacteria become less active or even die. To prevent this, media such as gravel, hair rollers and piping can be stirred and the disturbed debris drained and discarded. Foam media should be removed and rinsed in old pond water - the aim being to remove the worst of the debris but not the bacteria. Many external filters have a drain in the bottom of the biological section which, when opened will quickly draw water through the media and remove some debris. Even with these filters careful stirring of the media will be beneficial.

In all cases the biological filter medium should not be cleaned using tap water. Tap water contains chlorines and chloramines which have been added to kill bacteria and other organisms harmful to humans. If tap water is poured into the filter the chlorine in it will kill the helpful bacteria resulting in serious water quality problems.

The frequency of filter cleaning depends on a number of factors including water temperature, numbers of fish being kept and size of filter. An indication that cleaning is necessary is given when the filter outflow is reduced. This may involve cleaning the mechanical filter at

Successful pond maintenance is essential for koi, in this case a sanke, to remain at its best.

daily intervals during the summer. The biological media require less frequent cleaning, with once every 14-21 days being satisfactory during normal summer conditions. At temperatures below 8°C (when the fish stop feeding) regular cleaning is not necessary, and the disturbance caused can actually have an adverse effect on the fish.

Sand pressure filters present an unusual case. Due to the very fine particle size of the filter medium, these filters should be cleaned (ie back flushed) each day, with any dirty water being discarded.

Cleaning the Pump

The pump which services the filter is the heart of the pond and it is vital that it continues to run at all times in order to provide the oxygenated water which keeps the helpful bacteria active. Debris getting into the pump and caught around the impeller can cause damage and reduce the water output. To prevent this most pumps have some form of pre-filter which removes any coarse debris prior to it entering the pump. The pre-filter will require regular cleaning, sometimes several times a day if it is to allow a good flow of water through the pump. On a more occasional basis the pump itself should be unplugged, dismantled and cleaned following the instructions. The pump should be switched off for as short a time as possible, and never for more than 30 minutes to avoid killing the helpful bacteria.

Topping up the Pond

Freshwater has to be added to the pond occasionally to replace that lost through evaporation or during cleaning. For most koi keepers the replacement water will be from a household tap. If less than 5% of the pond volume is being added the chlorine present in the tap water should pose no problems if introduced correctly. The tap water should be sprayed into the air, which will result in the dissipation of a large proportion of the chlorine. The remainder will be dissolved at least 20 times in the pond water with no adverse effects on the fish. Small water changes administered in this way will also overcome any temperature changes and high metal levels.

When much more than 5% of the pond volume is being added it is advisable to use a good quality dechlorinator such as Tetra Pond AquaFin in order to remove the harmful chlorine. If chloramine is added to the water supply in your area, it will not be dissipated by spraying in the air, and a water conditioner should be used whenever water is added. Your local aquatic outlet or koi dealer should be able to advise you on this point.

Whenever adding new water never introduce it directly into the filter. Even if conditioned, the water may contain metals or be a different temperature which could adversely affect the helpful bacteria. If introduced into the pond it will be diluted manyfold and the slight changes in temperature and metal content which occur will have no adverse effects.

In some more advanced ponds a ball valve is used to automatically replace any water that is lost or removed from the pond. Such valves are best designed to replace the water slowly, so that the small amount of chlorine added is dissolved many times and so is not harmful. When more than 5% of the pond volume is to be replaced the use of a dechlorinator is advisable.

Water Quality Monitoring

The importance of good water quality was stressed in an earlier section in this guide.

By adopting the practices suggested in this book the quality of the water in your pond or aquarium should be suitable for koi keeping. However, routine monitoring of the water quality is essential in order to detect any changes or unsuitable conditions before they adversely affect the fish.

In an established, stable pond, Ammonia, Nitrite, Nitrate and pH levels should be measured at weekly intervals. Water hardness may be measured at 14 day intervals.

Where the pond is being altered in any way more frequent water testing is advisable. Following the introduction of new fish or a large filter clean out, daily monitoring of Ammonia, Nitrite and Nitrate is advisable. This should be continued for

2-3 days, or until the levels drop to their normal values. Water used in a large water change should also be tested for pH and nitrate to ensure that it is similar to that in the pond. These tests are inexpensive, but regular use of them is an essential part of pond maintenance and ensures that your fish remain healthy.

The Use of Salt

Salt (Sodium chloride) is frequently added to koi ponds on a regular basis with the aim of preventing disease outbreaks and generally "improving" conditions for the koi. When used as a constant addition to the pond, the salt actually has few beneficial effects and can cause the koi or the koi keeper some problems.

Salt is a good treatment for fungi and some other external diseases. However, when used continually, these parasites develop resistance to the salt and are not controlled by it. Salt does reduce the toxicity of nitrites, but should only be used temporarily in this role - until the cause of the high nitrites is detected and corrected. Finally salt reduces the intensity of the skin colouration of your koi giving them a paler appearance. In general, salt should not be routinely added to your pond, instead use it for emergencies.

Algal Problems

In most koi ponds problems arise from time to time as a result of algal growth. In many cases the trouble sorts itself out, but in others it is necessary to take remedial action.

Green Water

Green water is a problem that affects most koi ponds at some time, and, if you are unlucky, affects your pond every year for long periods. The green water is caused by minute green plants known as algae which occur in vast quantities when the conditions suit them (bright light and a plentiful supply of nutrients). In some cases, when you can only see 8-10cm under the water, there may be over 40,000 algae in every 5 millilitres (= 1 teaspoonful) of water! New ponds are particularly at risk, because the nutrients in the tap water provide ideal conditions for the algae.

Benefits

The algae do little harm to the fish, even when the water resembles pea soup. In fact they actually improve the condition of the fish by releasing essential vitamins and iodine into the water. These substances improve the overall health and vitality of the fish and result in a very intense colouration. Unfortunately in a green pond these benefits cannot be seen. However Tetra have formulated a water conditioner which provides the benefits of green water, without the green colouration. Tetra Koi Vital can be used in any pond, or even in an aquarium to bring out the best colouration in your koi (and goldfish) as well as improving their general health and vitality.

Dense suspended algal growth causing "green water" makes viewing the koi very difficult.

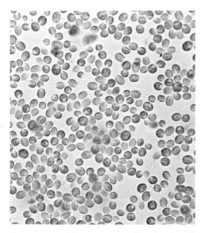

The cause of "green water" - algal cells viewed under the microscope.

Disadvantages

In certain circumstances the green water in the pond can cause problems to the fish. The millions of algae that are present in the water are all respiring, that is taking in oxygen and giving out carbon dioxide. On hot calm nights this can result in an oxygen shortage in the pond which, in severe cases can be fatal for the fish. If you notice your fish gasping under these conditions a partial water change coupled with increasing the water circulation using a fountain, pump or airstone should save them. Such events only occur infrequently and by far the greatest disadvantage with algae is the fact that they prevent the koi from being seen.

Control

There are several different ways of controlling algae, but one of the most successful is to kill the algae using a good quality algicide and then to prevent it returning by improving filtration, adding a vegetable filter or providing some form of shade.

Good quality algicides can be used to successfully treat the majority of algae found in garden ponds without damaging the fish or plants. However, it must be remembered that when the water appears green it contains many thousands of algae, and if these are all killed (when the algicide is added), they will all sink to the bottom of the pond and start to decompose, so polluting the water. To avoid this there are two courses of action which may be followed. The first is to change half of the pond water to remove the algae, and then treat the pond to prevent it returning. Alternatively the pond can be treated with algicide and left for several days for the dead algae to sink to the bottom before siphoning it out. Whichever option you choose, it is important to ensure that

An Ultra Violet light unit, commonly used to control suspended algae in the pond.

the algicide is evenly distributed in the pond following its application. This can be achieved by first diluting the required dose of algicide with water and then applying the solution evenly over the pond surface using a clean watering can. Avoid getting the algicide solution onto floating lily leaves as the strong solution can cause areas of the leaves to die.

Once the algae has been killed the pond keeper can concentrate on preventing it returning. This is achieved by altering the conditions in the pond so that they do not suit the algae, i.e. by removing the nutrients or the light that the algae requires to grow. Nutrients can be removed by installing a vegetable filter as described in the section on filtration. Shading can be achieved by adding surface dwelling plants such as lilies, by planting tall marginal species such as yellow flag iris or by covering the pond with a coarse mesh. If lilies can be used because if the koi are too small to uproot them, add sufficient to cover 50-70% of the water surface. Filtration can also be used to control algae by means of a very fine media (eg foam) which will mechanically strain out the algae, or a large settling chamber which enables them to sediment out of the water.

Many koi keepers have achieved great success in controlling green water by using an Ultra Violet (UV) Sterilising Unit incorporated into the pipework to or from the filter. The algae passing through these units are killed by the UV light produced. In order to maintain permanently clear water, it is important that you select a unit designed to treat the volume of water in your pond. When first installed the UV Steriliser will kill all of the algae within 2-3 days. To prevent these algae decomposing and polluting the water, undertake a partial water change and remove the dead material as soon as the pond has cleared. Without the algae to use up nitrates in your pond, it is likely that the nitrate level will increase. Regular monitoring using a Tetra Nitrate Test Kit is therefore advisable. If the nitrate reaches dangerous levels it is advisable to undertake frequent partial water changes and install or increase the size of your vegetable filter.

Blanketweed

Blanketweed is not in fact a weed, but is the collective name for several species of filamentous algae. As with the algae responsible for green water, the filamentous algae thrive in bright conditions where there are abundant nutrients. Where favourable conditions exist the blanketweed can grow at a phenomenal rate, doubling its own weight in only 24 hours. Blanketweed can often occur and prove troublesome in ponds where a UV steriliser had been installed. This is due to the large amounts of nutrients and light available which were previously used by the suspended algae.

Advantages

There are, perhaps surprisingly, a number of advantages in having blanketweed in your koi pond. Firstly, it will only occur in water where the ammonia, nitrite and nitrate concentrations are reasonably low, therefore its presence indicates that the conditions in the pond are suitable for your koi.

Blanketweed also absorbs ammonia-and nitrate from the water as a source of nutrition. Both of these substances are toxic to the koi at raised levels and so the algae actually improves the water conditions within the pond. If properly managed it will act as an ideal vegetable filter, removing the ammonia and nitrate that are produced as the fish waste decomposes. These nutrients would otherwise encourage suspended algae. It is very uncommon to find both blanketweed and green water in the same pond because the blanketweed out competes the suspended algae for the nutrients, thereby keeping the water clear. By removing the blanketweed on a

Blanket weed will take advantage of the nutrients and light present in a koi pond, resulting in rapid growth.

weekly basis you can therefore greatly reduce the pollutant levels in your pond, have clear water and maintain perfect water quality.

Koi are omnivorous, eating both plant and animal matter. This includes large quantities of filamentous algae if it is present. The blanketweed and the invertebrates which live within it provide an ideal source of food for the koi through the winter and whilst you are away on holiday.

Under the microscope blanket weed can be seen to be a mass of interwoven algal filaments.

Disadvantages

By far the greatest disadvantage with blanketweed is due to it choking everything in the pond. The algae filaments become entangled as they grow and if left unchecked, will block the filter, smother the plants and reduce the area in which the fish can swim. When present in such large quantities the blanketweed can greatly reduce the oxygen levels in the pond, particularly on still warm nights, when the algae photosynthesise rapidly and little oxygen is absorbed into the water. A further problem can arise in the autumn when the blanketweed, if not removed, starts to die and decompose so rapidly polluting the water.

Control

Before choosing a method for controlling blanketweed, the pondkeeper should consider the advantages and disadvantages in the pond in question, and then decide if eradication is necessary, or whether reducing the growth or using the blanketweed as a vegetable filter would be a better alternative.

There are a number of successful control methods which can be used:

1. Manual Clearance

Manual clearance is unlikely to completely remove the filamentous algae unless you drain and scrub the pond, sterilise the filter and throw away the plants. However, it can be kept under control through removal by hand, or by twisting it around a rake or stick. This method is quite successful in a koi pond. In mid-summer it can be a fruitless task, with the blanketweed re-growing very rapidly.

2. Algicides

Reliable algicides can be used to effectively eliminate blanketweed without damaging the koi. The death of large quantities of filamentous algae, followed by its decomposition can rapidly pollute the water and affect the fish. It is therefore advisable to combine algicide treatment with manual clearance. In this way you can remove as much algae as possible and then treat to prevent it returning.

If, despite this, you see signs of the fish gasping at the surface of the water, removing as much dead algae as possible combined with a partial water change should remedy the situation. When treated with an algicide, the algae stop growing, stop producing bubbles of oxygen and appear very stringy. Some fibrous species can remain green for some time, not because they are still alive, but simply because it takes several days (or even weeks) for them to decompose.

3. Use of a Vegetable Filter and Shading

Blanketweed requires the same conditions for growth as the algae responsible for green water. Therefore, by planting the vegetable filter with fast growing healthy plants (to remove excess nutrients) and covering the pond with some form of shading, the blanketweed growth can be greatly reduced.

A Combined Approach

Each of these methods of control can and has been used to successfully control blanketweed. However, using a combination of methods is perhaps the most successful once the blanketweed is established. A proven formula is to manually remove as much blanketweed as possible, treat with an algicide to kill the remaining shoots and then install a vegetable filter or shade the pond to prevent it returning.

A koi pond should look attractive and provide the ideal setting against which the fish can be viewed. The areas covered in this section should help you to achieve this aim. More details of when and how frequently they should be conducted is provided in the section on Seasonal Care.

Beautiful koi and clear water - the result of good pond maintenance.

SEASONAL GUIDE TO KOI CARE

If kept in an outdoor pool your koi will be influenced by the seasonal nature of the weather. This will in turn affect the timing of a number of routine tasks that need to be undertaken to keep both the koi and pond in good condition. The time of year when these tasks are undertaken depends largely on the locality in which you live and on the climate, therefore the months given in this chapter should only be used as a guideline. The activities of your fish and the pond conditions should provide a more accurate indication of when a particular task should be undertaken.

January/February

POND CONDITIONS At this time of year the pond water will be at its coldest, less than 6°C in most areas and possibly as low as 2-4°C. Ice may form on the top of the pond. The water is likely to be very clear due to the lack of algal growth.

KOI BEHAVIOUR The koi should be in a state of virtual hibernation and be seen to be motionless in the deepest part of the pond as this is where the warmest water will be. During mild spells in the weather the fish may become more active and be seen mouthing algae and other items in the pond. The fish

should not be disturbed unnecessarily as this will cause them to use up their valuable food reserves.

FEEDING The koi should not be fed when water temperatures are below 8°C. During prolonged mild spells the fish can be offered very small quantities of easily digested foods such as TetraPond Sticks. Ideally the fish should be fed in the morning to give them a chance to digest the food before the cooler evenings, but only feed if the fish are active and searching for food.

FILTER MAINTENANCE As indicated in the section on filtration, your filter should, in general be turned off in a planted pool. In a fish only pond the pump should be set to its lowest setting. The pump inflow and filter outflow should be close to the water surface to minimise water circulation. Throughout this period the filter will probably require a minimum of maintenance. Occasionally clean the mechanical filter section if debris starts to accumulate. In very cold weather it may be necessary to provide some insulation around external filters to prevent them freezing. A layer of "bubblewrap" or several layers of thick polythene supported on a wooden frame can be placed over filters which have been sunk into the ground. This arrangement should be placed 10 to 15cm above the surface of the filter so that the trapped air can act as an additional insulating layer. Filters placed above the ground in exposed areas may require an insulating layer on all surfaces. An aquarium heater placed in the first chamber (or all chambers) will help to prevent the water freezing.

POND MAINTENANCE Ice formation on the pond can pose problems by preventing gas exchange from the water surface. To prevent the ice forming over the entire pond a small floating pond heater can be added. This heater should be switched on whenever ice formation could occur. Most pondkeepers prevent ice formation by the use of an insulating layer as described above which is supported 15-30cm above the pond surface. Make sure it is secured correctly or the wind may damage or remove it. The cover should allow light to pass through so that any algae present in the pond photosynthesise and produce oxygen, rather than dying and polluting the water. For this reason if snow falls on the cover it should be removed as soon as possible. Equally, if ice is allowed to form on part of the pond and snow settles on it, it should be removed. The koi will be inactive in the deepest (and warmest) part of the pond at this time. A clean plastic dustbin or bucket placed on its side in this part of the pond will help to reduce wa-

ter circulation and maintain the warm water area. The koi will congregate in and around the dustbin or bucket, taking advantage of the warm water and avoiding any disturbance.

Throughout the winter your pond may be visited by hungry predatory birds, such as herons. A cover or net is the only sure way of preventing the heron attacking your fish. Other methods that can be successful include suspending strong nylon fishing line 30 and 45cm above ground level, all around the pond circumference. This method works on the principle that the heron will land away from the pond and walk towards it - only to be prevented by the fishing line. Unfortunately if very hungry the heron may overcome this barrier by landing directly in the water. Finally a plastic heron may be used. The theory here being that herons are territorial and will not feed close to another individual. However, in some cases the heron may not have read the rules!

March/April

POND CONDITIONS The days will begin to lengthen throughout this period. The air and water temperatures also start to rise. Algae and plants will respond to these conditions and start to grow. In many cases a bloom of suspended algae can occur resulting in green water conditions. Sudden tem-

perature changes may occur between day and night which could adversely affect the fish in shallow ponds.

KOI BEHAVIOUR The koi will become increasingly more active throughout this period and will start to feed. As the fish awaken from their semi-hibernation they may be weakened and susceptible to parasite infection. Watch out for the obvious signs of disease described in a previous chapter in this handbook. The worst affected individuals should be removed to a treatment container and treated with a suitable remedy. Make sure that the container is out of direct sunlight or the effects of a late frost, both of which may cause sudden and dangerous temperature changes. A garden shed or garage is ideal. It is also advisable to add the recommended dosage of a broad spectrum anti-parasite treatment such as TetraPond Medi-Fin as soon as the water temperature is over 10°C. This will counter raised parasite levels, before they adversely affect the fish.

FEEDING The koi will begin actively searching for food as soon as the water temperatures rise above 8°C. Initially they should be fed on small feeds of easily digested foods such as TetraPond Floating Foodsticks. Occasional feeds with safe live foods such as bloodworms and earthworms will also help to tempt the appetites of sluggish fish. The fish will not take great quantities of food initially so take care not to overfeed.

FILTER MAINTENANCE As the water temperature rises above 8°C the pump and filter should be restarted if they have been removed through the winter. It is advisable to monitor the ammonia and nitrite levels within the pond at this time to ensure they do not rise too high. The use of chemical filter media such as zeolite will help to overcome such problems.

Pumps which have been running throughout the winter may be slowly turned up to approximately half the maximum flow throughout these two months. The pump inflow can also be placed at or near to the pond bottom when the temperature is above 8°C. Check the cable and connections for the pumps to ensure there is no damage.

Insulation around the filter can be removed when the danger of frost has passed. It will now be necessary to undertake more regular filter maintenance. Be guided by the water flow through the filter and the build up of debris in the mechanical filter. Air supplies to the filter should be re-installed to ensure good oxygen supply for the bacteria.

page 82/83: Throughout the winter your pond may have a layer of ice on the surface. It is advisable to keep an area ice free using a pond heater or cover.

The koi will start to feed as soon as the water temperature rises above 8°C.

POND MAINTENANCE After the danger of frost has receded the pond heater (if used) and/or insulation cover can be removed, cleaned and stored in readiness for next year.

If there has been a build up of filamentous algae or debris throughout the winter it should be removed to get the pond into ideal condition for the forthcoming season. The buckets or dustbin may be removed.

Algal problems will probably occur in ponds not using an ultra violet unit, due to the algae taking advantage of the raised light and nutrient levels before the plants in the pond or vegetable filter start growing. Suitable control measures may be implemented, as outlined in the chapter on Pond Management.

Regular water testing, particularly for ammonia and nitrite, is advisable to enable corrective measures to be taken should raised levels develop as the filter bacteria become more active. If ammonia or nitrite levels increase to dangerous levels a large partial water change will provide immediate relief.

May/June

POND CONDITIONS Water temperatures should still be rising throughout this period with values in excess of 15°C occurring in most regions. Algae will be growing rapidly unless controlled. Aquatic plants, if present will be flourishing and water lilies will start to flower.

KOI BEHAVIOUR The koi should now be active and feeding well. Towards the end of this period, if temperatures are above 18-20°C, the fish may begin to spawn. If you wish to keep the fry the necessary precautions should be taken ranging from collecting the eggs, to adding a spawning net. If spawning occurs in the pond check the fish to ensure they have not accidentally damaged themselves. Daily water testing for ammonia and nitrite is also advisable as decaying eggs can pollute the water.

FEEDING The koi will be feeding actively and should be offered a good quality food several times each day.
Higher protein foods such as TetraPond Koi Sticks and, at higher temperatures, TetraPond Growth Food for Koi are ideal. If you wish to breed your koi select the parents and condition them using higher protein foods.

FILTER MAINTENANCE The filter should be functioning well at the raised temperatures and should maintain negligible pollutant levels. Turn the pump up to its maximum flow rate to ensure efficient filtration. Regular cleaning will be necessary. Weekly testing of the ammonia, nitrite and nitrate values is still advisable. If an ultra violet unit is used to control suspended algal growth the nitrate levels in the pond may start to rise suggesting the need for partial water changes or an improved vegetable filter. The vegetable filter will be flourishing and it may be necessary to thin the plants, particularly if watercress has been used.

POND MAINTENANCE Regular partial water changes and/or the removal of debris will be necessary to prevent your koi disturbing it and clouding the water. Algal growth (suspended or filamentous) may be a problem and should be controlled as described in the section on pond maintenance. Blossom from trees in and around the pond can land in the pond and should be removed using a hand net. If it becomes a problem a fine net spread over the pond will be worthwhile for the short time that the blossom is present.
If plants are present in the pond they should now be growing actively. Make sure that they cannot be up-

rooted by the koi, which will feed on any new shoots.

Pond additives such as Tetra Koi Vital may be added on a regular basis throughout the summer and early autumn. They will enhance the colouration of your fish and improve vitality.

Floating debris may accumulate on the pond surface. This may be removed using a fine net, a skimmer which feeds surface water into the filter, or by using an overflow system.

Observe the koi when you feed them, watching for signs of disease or damage. Ulceration can be a particular problem following the rigours of spawning.

July/August

POND CONDITIONS Water temperatures will be at their maximum and should average 18-20°C in all but the most northerly regions. Your pond and koi should be looking at their best at this time of year.

KOI BEHAVIOUR Your koi will be at their most active throughout this period. Spawning is possible when the water temperature rises above 18-20°C and the necessary precautions should be taken. If water temperatures rise above 25°C the koi will become lethargic and are unlikely to feed. Gasping at the water surface may occur on hot still

Dense algal growth resulting in "green water" can occur throughout the warmer months, particularly if there are no plants and a vegetable filter is not used.

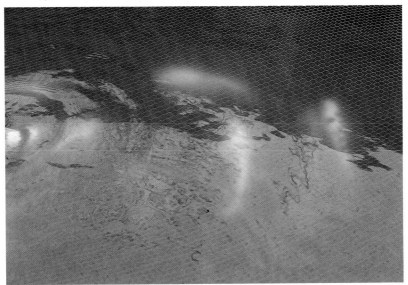

A fine net spread over the pond will not detract from its beauty and will prevent blossom or leaves falling into the water.

nights, particularly if plants and dense algal growth is present in the pond.

FEEDING The fish will be feeding ravenously because of the high water temperatures. To encourage healthy growth you should be feeding the koi at least twice a day and include a high protein good such as TetraPond Growth Food for koi in the diet. A whole clean lettuce can be placed in the pond in the evenings if large koi are kept and will almost certainly have been eaten by morning.

Any koi fry should be fed several times a day on a finely powdered food followed by a flaked diet as they grow.

Treat foods can be given by hand at this time of the year and will quickly result in your koi becoming very tame.

FILTER MAINTENANCE Regular (perhaps daily) filter cleaning may be necessary throughout the warm period of the year due to the large amounts of fish waste produced. If not already present, air stones may be placed into the biological sections of the filter to add oxygen and improve the efficiency of the filter bacteria. The bacteria and other life in the filter will consume large amounts of oxygen. To re-oxygenate the water before it enters the pond ensure it passes through a venturi or down a waterfall. Sand pressure filters should be back flushed on a daily basis. The vegetable filter will still be growing rapidly and will require thinning.

POND MAINTENANCE If water temperatures rise above 25-27°C the fish will probably stop feeding and become more lethargic. Some form of shading over the pond may be necessary to prevent the pond becoming too hot - coarse netting or greenhouse shading can be used to good effect. Sunburn can also be a problem if the koi are in a clear water without any form of shading. This will often show up as skin damage on the upper surface of the body, but can easily be prevented using the shading.

Watch out for signs of low oxygen levels in the pond particularly if well planted or containing "green" water. Such problems usually occur in the early morning when the weather is hot and still and are indicated by gasping at the water surface. Conditions can be quickly improved by aerating the water using a waterfall, fountain, venturi or airstone. In severe cases, or if your pond does not have these additions changing 5-10% of the water will help.

Regular removal of debris from the pond bottom will be necessary if this is not done automatically using the pump and/or drainage system. Failure to do so can result in the koi disturbing any debris and clouding the water. Also the debris may release nutrients which will encourage algal growth.

September/October

POND CONDITIONS Water temperatures within the pond will gradually reduce during these months. Large air temperature fluctuations may occur due to the warm days and cold, frosty nights. This should have little effect on deep koi ponds, but could influence the temperature in small shallow ponds. Plants and filamentous algae should start to die back. In many ponds a bloom of suspended algae may occur, taking advantage of the nutrients which are not now being used by the vegetable filter. Such blooms are usually short lived and the water will clear for the rest of the winter.

KOI BEHAVIOUR The koi will still be active and feeding. This activity will decrease in October as water temperatures reduce. The koi will be at their most attractive at this time of year due to the cooler temperatures intensifying colouration. The use of pond additives will further improve this colouration.

FEEDING Feeding should be reduced in accordance with the koi's smaller appetites. Higher protein foods should not be given when the water temperature falls below 15°C. TetraPond Koi and Floating Food Sticks will be ideal throughout this time. In the autumn the koi are building up food reserves to last them through the winter, so ensure the food given is of high quality.
Koi fry will be feeding actively and should reach lengths of up to 18cm before they stop searching for food. Treat foods should only be given above a temperature of 12-15°C.

FILTER MAINTENANCE Regular cleaning will still be necessary throughout this period. The plants in the vegetable filter may start to die back and should be trimmed or removed all together. Regular water quality testing is advisable to ensure that this does not cause raised levels of pollutants. Towards the end of this period when the fish become less active, the pump should be turned down to two thirds of its maximum flow rate.

POND MAINTENANCE This is an ideal time to give the pond its annual overhaul and remove any debris or algae that has accumulated through the summer. The cleaning is best done before the water temperature falls below 10°C as the fish will still be actively feeding and their immune system working so minimising any ill effects from the disturbance. The dead or decaying leaves of any aquatic plants should be removed at this time to prevent future water pollution.

page 90/91: Throughout the summer a pergola will shade the pond preventing overheating and reducing algal growth.

Leaf fall at this time of year can be a particular problem if there are any trees in the vicinity. A fine net should be placed across the pond in order to prevent them landing in the pond. The net will also help to deter herons and other koi predators. A routine treatment with a broad spectrum anti parasite treatment such as TetraPond MediFin is advisable to reduce parasite numbers prior to the winter.

November/December

POND CONDITIONS Water temperatures will drop considerably, often to values as low as 2-4°C. Air temperatures may fall to freezing point resulting in the formation of ice on some parts of the pond. At these temperatures any plants and algae will have died back, resulting in the water appearing very clear.

KOI BEHAVIOUR As the water temperatures decrease the koi will gradually become less active and are likely to stop feeding and become very lethargic. During mild periods the koi will actively search for food whilst, in contrast, they will remain motionless on the pond bottom during the cold spells. The fish should not be disturbed unnecessarily as this will cause them to use up valuable food reserves.

FEEDING Only feed the fish when the water temperature is above 8°C and take care not to overfeed.

An insulating cover over the pond will help to prevent the water temperature falling too low. (Photograph courtesy of R. Cleaver).

93

One feed per day should suffice. In general only low protein foods which are easy to digest (eg Tetra Pond Food Sticks) should be given. If temperatures are just above 8°C but are likely to drop within a few hours due to cold weather conditions the fish should not be fed.

FILTER MAINTENANCE Turn the pump down to its lowest flow rate and raise the filter inflow and outflow to minimise water circulation. In planted ponds the filter may be removed and the pump cleaned and serviced before storing. At this time of year it is also advisable to clean the filter and pipework to remove any debris that has accumulated throughout the year (despite the routine maintenance). If an air pump has been used to inject air into the filter, it should be moved indoors or switched off, to prevent cold air being pumped into the filter system. If freezing is expected, place some form of insulation on and around the filter - some koi keepers place an aquarium heater in the filter to prevent the water freezing.

Occasional cleaning of the mechanical filter media may be necessary if debris accumulates. Otherwise very little upkeep will be required.

POND MAINTENANCE The pond should require little maintenance during this period. Due to the low water temperatures the koi should not be disturbed therefore take care if debris needs to be removed from the pond. The anti-predator net should be left in place if there is any threat to the koi. This may be replaced by an insulating cover if ice formation is a possibility. A pond heater may also be required if the weather turns cold early in the winter. If any fish show signs of disease it will be necessary to remove them to a separate container for treatment. Before treating, the water should very slowly be raised to above 10°C (over a period of 5-7 days using an aquarium heater) to ensure that the remedies are effective. It is wise to keep the fish in this container until March/April when the pond begins to warm up.

BUYING AND HANDLING KOI

Buying koi for your pond can be a very exciting time, but can also lead to disaster if you are not careful. A number of factors need to be considered before you buy a koi and attempt to transport it home.

Sources of Koi

Koi are now being produced throughout the world, although the major breeding countries are in Japan, Israel, USA and Singapore. Japan is the home of the koi and the best quality fish are, without a doubt, produced here. Unfortunately good quality Japanese koi have a high price tag attached to them and so are too expensive for many koi keepers. Home bred koi and those from the other breeding countries are improving each year and often represent excellent value.

Koi Outlets

Koi can be purchased from a selection of different outlets ranging from small general pet stores to specialist koi centres. Before buying your koi from any of these sources it is important to check that the fish are being kept in good health. If the fish are unhealthy or the ponds show signs of negligence (eg cloudy water, excess debris, uneaten food or overcrowding) you would be wise not to buy any koi. Koi bought from

A koi auction room in Japan. Boxes of koi are floated between rows of buyers from around the world.

such an outlet are often stressed by the conditions in which they are kept, which can lead to disease problems when you introduce them into your own pond or aquarium. It is advisable to seek a knowledgeable and reputable dealer. Such a person will be able to offer invaluable advice on the koi you intend to purchase and also on any pond problems should they develop in the future.

When to buy

Koi are available for sale throughout the year from most garden centres and koi dealers.

It is important, however, that you only buy fish for your pond when it, and the fish within it are in good condition. It is pointless buying a new koi if there are disease or water quality problems within your pond. A new koi being introduced into such an environment would be unlikely to survive for long. Instead you should correct the problem and leave the pond for a few weeks to ensure that everything is satisfactory before you buy the koi. If you have found a koi that you particularly like, but your pond or fish are not in good condition, a small deposit will usually retain the fish until you are ready.

High quality koi tend to be exported from Japan in the period from Oc-

tober to December. This is the season when the growing on ponds at koi farms are drained and the fish harvested. A wide selection of very good koi can be seen during this period particularly if you find out when new fish are to be imported and visit your dealer soon afterwards. Many of these koi will be bought soon after they arrive in the dealers ponds, but will only be introduced into hobbyists ponds in the spring, when water temperatures start to rise and the fish will settle more easily.

Koi auctions are an ideal place at which to buy fish when establishing a pond. These auctions are becoming increasingly popular with the major koi dealers as a way of selling koi before the next batch is imported.

At such auctions you should take advantage of the viewing period to select fish which you wish to bid for in order to check them for any signs of poor health or damage. To ensure you only select, and bid for, healthy fish it is wise to ask an experienced friend to go along with you to view the koi.

Bargains are often available at these auctions, but don't be tempted to buy unhealthy or damaged fish or purchase too many at one time. After all a koi is only good value if it survives.

page 96 /97: At the koi actions in Japan large numbers of fish are sold. In the photograph each box contains one "lot" of fish for auction

Koi Selection

The colour or variety of koi you select is a matter of personal choice. The points to consider when selecting a good quality specimen differ according to the variety. Points to look for are outlined in "The Tetra Encyclopedia of Koi" published by Tetra and "Modern Nishikigoi - Basic varieties and Unique Koi" by Takeo Kuraki published by Shin Nippon Tasho.

Of particular importance when selecting a koi is the fact that it should be in good health. You should spend some time watching and examining the koi before you decide to buy.

Unhealthy fish often exhibit the following characteristics and should be avoided:

Fins clamped against the body
Obvious parasites
Physical Damage
Gasping or rapid gill movements
Rubbing against underwater objects
Emaciated appearance (thin head and body)
Sulking away from other individuals
Gill covers held away from the body
Pale slimy appearance over the body and eyes.

Having selected a koi which appears healthy you should ask the dealer to let you have a closer look. With larger fish this will involve carefully netting the koi and placing it in a suitable bowl or basket. If you are still interested in the koi ask for it to be placed in a polythene bag which will allow you to carefully view the underside.

Upon closer examination you may be able to see larger parasites or any physical damage. Pay attention to the base of the fins and the vent, if reddened this may indicate an internal infection.

Most dealers will be willing to capture individual fish for you to examine more closely. Do not ask to look at any that you are not seriously considering buying as the capturing stresses the koi, as well as the dealer!

Transportation

Once you have selected your koi the dealer will place it into a polythene bag one third filled with water from the pond. The bag will then be inflated with oxygen and sealed. The oxygen is more important to the koi than the water and will ensure that it does not suffocate on the journey home. In many cases the koi will be placed in two or even three bags to avoid accidents and prevent leaks. If you are "bagging" you own fish always select a polythene bag which is large enough to accommodate the koi without it bending. Sufficient water should be added from the pond so that it just covers the gills. If the fish are to be transported for more than 60 minutes, or in hot conditions it is wise to use oxygen to inflate the bag. For shorter journeys air will be adequate. When sealing the bag twist the loose end of the polythene bag (not the full end) in

Koi are available in a multitude of colours and varieties. It is important that you choose fish which appeal to you.

order to trap the oxygen. The twisted part of the bag can then be sealed using an elastic band.

The polythene bag containing the koi should be carried and transported in a way that will avoid the fish bending. For larger fish this usually means carrying the bag on its side. To minimise stress on the journey home it is advisable to place the bag in a cardboard or better still a polystyrene box. This will prevent unnecessary rolling and help to minimise sudden temperature and light changes. In the car place the box so that it cannot move, ideally in the boot.

Wherever possible the box should be placed so that the koi points towards one side of the car, as this will minimise disturbance.

Introducing the Koi

Once home the bag containing the koi should be gently floated on the pond surface in order for the water temperature in the bag to change to that in the pond. This will generally take 30 to 40 minutes, but it is advisable to check using a thermometer before the fish is released. Once the temperatures are the same the bag can be opened and the fish allowed to swim into the pond. If the koi has been in a polythene bag for several hours it is worth carefully releasing the fish and then discarding as much of the water as

p. 100/101: A Japanese koi farm - the best quality koi are still produced in Japan.

When catching large koi for inspection always try to avoid lifting them out of the water. (Photograph courtesy of R Cleaver).

possible. This water will be rich in organic waste material and could overburden the filter particularly in a quarantine container.

Handling Koi

In general your koi should not be handled except when absolutely necessary.

This is because netting and particularly handling, the koi can lead to the delicate skin or fin membranes being damaged and left open to infection.

If it is necessary to net your koi for example to transfer them to a treatment container try not to lift them clear of the water. Instead catch the fish in a soft meshed, shallow net and carefully place them into a partly submerged container. With care this can be achieved without the fish coming out of the water.

If handling is necessary, for example to place the fish into a polythene bag you must try to prevent the fish from struggling and damaging itself. This can be achieved by holding the fish with its head pointing towards you. One hand should be placed underneath the jaw of the fish, gently holding the fish around the abdomen behind the gills. The fish should appear to be resting its head on the underside of your wrist. The other hand is placed on the underside of the fish around the vent. The fish may than be quickly moved from one container to the next.

Handling and transporting koi can cause severe damage if done incorrectly, therefore it is wise to ask an experienced koi keeper or a dealer to demonstrate how it should be done before you attempt it yourself using the guidelines above.

KOI KEEPING IN AQUARIA

Koi are not ideal fish to keep in an aquarium as they will quickly outgrow all but the largest tanks. There are, however, occasions when they can be kept in the aquarium for short periods. Koi fry for example, may be overwintered in an indoor aquarium in order to protect them from severe weather conditions. Small koi may also be "grown on" in the warmer aquarium conditions before being introduced into the pond. Additionally, small koi may be quarantined or treated in a suitably sized aquarium.

If, for whatever reason, it is necessary to keep koi in an aquarium a number of points should be considered.

Size of the aquarium
In general you should use an aquarium which is at least 60 x 30 x 30cm and preferably larger. The larger volume of water in such an aquarium will simplify maintenance, accommodate more fish and allow them to grow to a larger size.

The aquarium itself must always be positioned on a sturdy stand. Each litre of water weighs 1kg (1 gallon weighs 10lbs), therefore a 60 x 30 x 30cm aquarium plus gravel will weigh approximately 115kg (250lbs).

The position of the aquarium is important. It must be away from draughts, windows and room heaters as they will all cause large temperature fluctuations which will adversely affect the koi and particularly any fry. The tank must also be sited away from direct sunlight which will cause unsightly algal growth.

Lighting
Most aquariums are designed so that a cover or hood can be incorporated. The hood has a number of functions, including stopping evaporation, preventing dust and intruders (eg cats and children) reaching the water, and stopping the fish jumping out. The last function is particularly important where koi are being treated or quarantined.

An inexpensive hood can be made from a sheet of glass or perspex cut to size, however, if you intend to use artificial lighting a more elaborate design will be necessary. Commercially available hoods usually have fittings for fluorescent lighting. This form of illumination is probably the most suitable and economical for a coldwater aquarium. One light tube, slightly shorter than the length of the aquarium is suitable for viewing the fish, but if you wish to grow aquatic plants 15 watts per $900cm^2$ of water surface area will be necessary. A "white" or "daylight" fluorescent tube is the most suitable for illuminating your aquarium.

A clear condensation tray should be

Large, high quality koi like this Ki Utsuri are not suited to life in an aquarium.

placed between the water surface and the lighting in order to prevent condensation forming on electrical contacts.

Heating

Heating the aquarium is not necessary in most cases. However if the water temperature regularly falls below 10°C an aquarium heater may be added. The heater should be adjusted to raise the water temperature to 15-18°C.

Filtration

It is very important to maintain good water quality within the aquarium. This can prove difficult due to the relatively small volume of water contained in the aquarium, therefore adequate filtration is essential.

Undergravel filtration is very popular among tropical fishkeepers, but is not suitable for the coldwater aquarium. The koi will dig in the gravel more or less continually in their search for food, and in doing so will disturb any debris that has been sucked in to the substrate, causing the water to become cloudy. With larger koi it is not uncommon for the undergravel filter plates to be exposed by this digging thus short circuiting the filter and reducing its efficiency.

Electrically driven canister filters positioned either inside or outside the aquarium (depending on their design) are the most suitable form of filtration. These filters remove any debris from the aquarium so that it cannot be disturbed by the koi. Canister filters can be filled with a variety of filter media, but for most circumstances a foam block is ideal. In larger external filters a coarse prefilter such as a nylon pad can be added. Chemical filter media (such as charcoal or better still zeolite) are also useful as they will help to prevent raised pollutant levels, particularly in newly set up aquaria.

Foam filters are useful in aquaria containing koi fry. In this situation a canister filter would suck in the fry and so would be unsuitable. Foam filters are also useful in quarantine or treatment aquaria, as they can easily be removed for cleaning.

Filter size is important and you should select a model which will circulate 1 to 2 times the tank volume each hour. If this creates excessive turbulence in the aquarium, direct the filter outflow downwards, against an underwater object or against the side of the tank. Water flow is desirable in moderation and will help to exercise the fish and prevent them becoming too rounded and fat.

Aquarium Decor

Choice of decoration in a koi aquarium is obviously a matter for the individual. It can vary from a layer of gravel with one or two stones, to a well planted set-up, or one containing pottery frogs, underwater galleons and plastic skeletons.

Aquarium gravel is available in a

range of sizes and colours. A 2 to 5 cm layer of pea sized natural gravel is ideal for most koi aquaria. Aim to slope the gravel towards the filter inflow so that the debris is removed. Rockwork, if used, should be firmly seated in the gravel to stop the koi digging and making it unstable. Avoid sharp rocks or those containing limestone which may injure the koi or adversely affect the water chemistry.

Plants, whether plastic or live, make an ideal background against which you can view the fish. Live plants are only suitable in aquaria containing small koi. Larger individuals (10 cm or greater) will uproot and eat most plants. Plastic plants are now more realistic than ever, and can be firmly anchored to prevent them from being uprooted.

Stocking the Tank

It is important to avoid overstocking the aquarium as this will reduce growth rates, encourage disease and result in poor water quality. As a guide you should allow 2.5cm of fish length for every 75cm^2 of aquarium water surface area. Care must be taken when fry or small fish are being "grown on" in the aquarium as it can rapidly become overstocked as the fish grow.

Feeding

The koi in your aquarium should be fed on the same diet that they would be given in the pond. Fry may be fed initially with the microscopic animals found in matured pond water, which should be added 3 to 4 times each day. After 1 - 2 days the fry will accept Tetra Baby Fish Food for Egglayers. This may be given 3 to 5 times each day but take great care not to overfeed and pollute the water.

Above a length of 1.5cm, the small koi will readily accept flaked foods. TetraFin Goldfish Flakes and Tetra

Keeping koi in an aquarium allows them to be viewed from the side.

Growth Food are ideal and should be given 2 to 3 times daily. Above 10cm in length the koi will accept stick type food. Good growth and colouration can be achieved using TetraPond Growth Food for Koi and TetraPond Koi Sticks.

Routine Maintenance

Regular aquarium and filter maintenance is the secret to keeping good water conditions and therefore healthy koi. Even when small, koi tend to be messy feeders, therefore weekly aquarium and filter cleaning is advisable. Each week remove 10 to 20% of the water together with any debris that has accumulated in the aquarium and gravel. The gravel can easily be cleaned without clouding the water by using a Tetra Hydroclean Gravel Washer. The re-

placement water should be the same temperature as that in the aquarium and should be dechlorinated using Tetra AquaSafe.

At each partial water change the filter should also be cleaned. To do this remove the filter media and rinse in old aquarium water. Do not use tap water as the chlorine present will kill the helpful filter bacteria.

On an occasional basis the aquarium glass may need cleaning in order to remove algal growth. This can be achieved using algae scrapers or filter wool. The condensation tray may also require cleaning to ensure that sufficient light passes through for viewing or to encourage plant growth.

Water Testing

The relatively small volumes of water in an aquarium can result in quite rapid changes in water quality. It is therefore advisable to undertake regular water quality tests. Ammonia and nitrite are perhaps the most important parameters and should be tested at weekly intervals, or more frequently if fish have recently been added or if the aquarium is new. pH and Nitrate may also cause problems and should be tested at two weekly intervals. It is advisable to test all new tap water for nitrate and pH before it is introduced into the aquarium in order to avoid sudden changes. This is particularly important if fry are present.

Maintaining koi in an aquarium can add a new dimension to your hobby of koi keeping. It will allow you to purchase small, good quality fish and grow them into larger specimens before introducing them into your pond. Raising the fry that you have bred can also prove very rewarding, and enables you to continue your hobby throughout the winter, when the adult fish in the pond are inactive and best left alone.

Within an aquarium overcrowding or overfeeding can quickly lead to water cloudiness.

FURTHER INFORMATION

The following publications contain useful information on all aspects of koi keeping.

Books

"A Fishkeepers Guide to Koi" by B James, published by Tetra
"A Fishkeepers Encyclopedia of Koi" published by Tetra
"Modern Nishikigoi - Basic Varieties and Unique Koi" by Takeo Kuroki, published by Shin Nippon Kyoiku Tosho
"Manual to Nishikigoi" by Takeo Kuroki, published by Shin Nippon Kyoiku Tosho
"The Cult of the Koi" by M Tamadachi, published by TFH
"The Fishkeepers Manual of Fish Health" by Andrews, Exell and Carrington published by Tetra

Magazines

"Nishikigoi International" - a specialist koi magazine published quarterly and available on subscription from Nishikigoi International Ltd, 7 Canterbury Avenue, Lowton, Warrington, Cheshire, WA3 2HA, United Kingdom.

"Rinko" - a specialist koi magazine produced in Japan - available from leading Koi dealers.
"Practical Fishkeeping" - published monthly and containing some articles on Koi keeping. Available from your newsagent or on subscription from Practical Fishkeeping, PO Box 500, Leicester, LE99 0AA, United Kingdom.

"Aquarist and Pondkeeper" published monthly and containing some articles on koi keeping. Available from newsagents, aquatic stores or on subscription from Aquarist and Pondkeeper, 9 Tufton Street, Ashford, Kent, TN23 1QN.

In addition koi keepers can receive invaluable information and meet people with similar interests by joining a local koi society. Relevant societies in the UK include "The British Koi Keepers Society" (which has sections throughout the country), "The Yorkshire Koi society" and "The Midland Koi Society". In the USA you may wish to join the "American Koi Society" which again has regional groups. "The Australian Koi Society" is the group to join in Australia. Each of these societies produce excellent magazines which will enable you to keep abreast of current trends in the world of koi keeping. Contact names and addresses for each society are not included here as they may change with time. However, your local koi dealer will be able to provide you with the current name and address of the secretaries of societies in your region.

BIOGRAPHY

The author, Dr David Pool, has been keeping fish for over 20 years and is well known for his radio interviews, TV appearances, lectures and magazine articles on the subiect. After obtaining an Honours Degree in Zoology he was awarded a PhD for his studies on the diseases of koi. He subsequently lectured at Liverpool University and Liverpool Polytechnic in Animal Parasitology and Fisheries Biology. In 1985 Dr Pool became a consultant to Tetra and headed the Information Centre which provides advice to thousands of fishkeepers every year.